Simon Ships Out

How one brave, stray cat became a worldwide hero

Jacky Donovan

Simon's quirkily humorous yet emotional cat's eye narrative is based on a true story. With the exception of those named below - listed in order of appearance within the book - all characters' names in this work are fictitious and any resemblance to real persons, living or dead, is purely coincidental.

Ordinary Seaman George Hickinbottom
Petty Officer George Griffiths
Lieutenant Commander Ian Griffiths
First Lieutenant Geoffrey L. Weston
Lieutenant Commander K. Stewart Hett
Lieutenant Commander Bernard Skinner
Telegraphist Jack French
Lieutenant Commander Jock Strain
Flight Lieutenant Michael Fearnley RAF
Lieutenant Commander John S. Kerans
Telegraphist Robert 'Bob' Ernest Stone

Simon Ships Out: How one brave, stray cat became a worldwide hero is as accurate as practicable based on available reports. With a sprinkling of artistic licence given that the four-legged crew below were, until now, unable to tell their side of the tale!

Simon the cat
Peggy the dog
Mao Tse Tung the rat
Hugo the rabbit

Contents

Prologue

I am curled up next to JoJo and telling him I have nine. He is laughing and saying I only have one. I can feel his heart thudding, thudding. I can hear it too, really hear it. His beating heart gets louder and louder until suddenly his heart must burst because - bang! I am jolted right off the bed and onto the floor.

All the others must hear it too because they spring up out of their beds. What *is* this? I dash out onto the deck and run up to the bow. Huge, scary flies are whizzing over my head and hitting the ship. I scamper up onto the bridge to try and escape them. The Captain is in there, Conway and Welburn at the wheel.

'I do believe someone's firing at us.' The Captain looks and sounds surprised. 'Action stations. Raise the battle ensign,' he barks and some of the men leap over me and quickly rush away. A horrible sound echoes all around the ship; the loudest, saddest wail I have ever heard. It makes my whole body shake and hurts my ears, my head. Make it stop.

Another huge bang and crash and I am thrown right across the bridge. I try to stand up, but I can't. Even though I can put my front paws onto the floor, my back legs don't move. Everything underneath me has tilted and there is thick, black smoke coming in from outside. It gets up my nose and makes my eyes sting. There is a screaming noise between my ears. I shake my head and try to stand. It is getting darker, hotter. There is a nasty, burning smell too. I cannot see or hear. It is hard to even breathe. I sit hunched; my whiskers, my ears, my fur, everything is standing on end. The Captain is lying on the floor. Welburn has fallen onto the wheel. What's happening?

Painfully, I lift myself up and slowly manage to crawl through the doorway, feeling my way out. It is easier to breathe, but I am panting. I can just about make out some shapes through the smoke. I see Conway lying down. He looks asleep. How funny. I give him a quick sniff, crawl round him and out onto the deck. It is very wet and slippery and, even though my back legs still hurt, I manage to drag myself slowly forwards. I hear another huge bang and see some men fall down, others running across the deck, through the horrible, thick smoke. It makes my eyes sting even more and hurts my throat.

I crawl out of the bridge to try and get away from the noise, but it is even louder out here. Another bang over the wailing; a thud and the ship tilts again. I look up at sky that is full of smoke to see if I can see any of the planes with the streaming tails flying overhead. Maybe this is pretend, like back home? As I watch the men unfold a large sheet there is another bang and two of the men fall down. I don't think this is pretend and if it is then it is not much fun. It must be real. The sheet the men unroll is a flag. They hang it over the side of the ship. Even though I know what a flag is, I don't know why they are doing it now. It seems a strange time to unroll a flag just to show where you are from.

Maybe I should just hide until the noise stops and the smoke and the banging go away. Where can I hide though? How can I escape this terrible noise that is hurting my ears; the horrible smoke that smells and stings just as much? No, if this is real then I want to be brave, need to be brave. Where are all the bangs coming from? And why? Slowly, I crawl up to the bow and look out. Thick, dirty-looking smoke hangs above the water. I gaze out across it and try to see through it.

The smoke clears a little over the water and I think I can make out Some kind of dark shape. I keep on looking to try and work out what it is. It is a ship, smaller than this one, with lots of men on it. So why are they doing this if they are the same as us? At that moment, amongst the men, I spot another shape, something small and fuzzy. It is moving around between their legs. It glances up and I spy one glinting green eye staring right back at me. Oh no! It can't be, can it...?

Another bang explodes in my ears, making them scream again. My legs hurt, my ears hurt, all of me hurts. I think I see Peggy and I try to make some kind of sound, but I can't. The bright noise of everything is closing in on me. I feel as if I am getting smaller, closing in on myself. I cannot tell if the screaming is inside or outside my head. The pain from my back legs is creeping up my side, down into my front paws. My head is heavy. It drops and I fall sideways onto the deck. The brightness turns to black, the screaming replaced...

By silence.

1/ Sky and land

One year earlier

The birds are flying high, high, high and swooping low above the port. Look - there's a brown booby and, just coming now, a loon ready to dive. A red footed booby goes round and round above me before landing on a rail. If they are here then that means it will be getting even more hot soon and, when that happens, a lot of the birds will fly away from the harbour.

I wish I could fly away.

The blast of a horn makes me twitch and blink away the picture of me flying. How funny. Maybe I would like to fly just for a little bit to see what it was like, but not all the time. I like my paws. And I certainly wouldn't want to fly away forever. Even when I look up at all of the birds high in the bright, bright sky and I know they can go wherever they want to, I know this is the one life I have and the one life I want. It is *my* life and I know this is where I want to be. I don't want to be anywhere else. Why would I?

There is the port for one thing. It is always full of huge ships, big and even more big, coming in from the big sea and others going away. Different colours, gleaming white or grey like dark time. Some have funnels on them and many of them have sheets tied to the mast. Although I can't make out all the different colours, I know the sheets are really called flags. The flags on the ships mean the ships come from places all over the world. They sail in from the big sea that connects all the places up. In between the huge ships are more small ones. Just like the birds, they have different names too: sampans and junks, tug boats and frigates.

And the other thing is JoJo of course. He told me the names of everything I know. The names of the birds and the boats and everything

3

else. JoJo is my big brother. He told me the birds come here because it is a good place to swim and dive and play. But really they come here because there are lots and lots and lots of fish. And that means lots of lovely food for them. JoJo thinks I should creep up behind one of the birds when they have landed on a jetty and I should pounce on it and then it could be food for me too. But I really don't want to do that. Or I should put my paw into the water's edge and try to catch a fish with my claws. But I don't want to do that either. And besides, I don't really like to get my paws or my ears or my tail wet. Not if I can help it. No thank you.

JoJo laughs at me when I tell him that. But I don't want to stop the birds flying. Or the little fish from being able to swim. I like to sit here on my jetty and watch them all; the fish darting about beneath me, the birds screeching and squawking above, all of them happy to be free. Maybe they're singing. I don't know. Sometimes when JoJo and I sing at night, a woman shouts at us to stop, which always makes us laugh. Once she even threw a bucket of water at us. It made me very wet, but not JoJo. That made him laugh even more. Not me though.

Often, men and women go out in their boats to catch fish too and they always leave a few in nets or buckets when they come back. Some of the smiling ones even throw them to me if I sit on a jetty and wait for them at dark time. I don't think even JoJo knows that. He is always too busy exploring and, even though I like to go with him, I also like to just sit here. Or lie down. In the sun, stretch my legs out. Feel the heat warm my fur even more as I lie on my back and just… streeetch.

Sometimes, after I've waited for the smiling men and women to throw me some fish when it is dark, or before JoJo and I settle down to sing for the night, he might want me to go with him so he can show me somewhere new he has found. So we trot along the harbour, jump up the steps - two, four, five - turn into the alley and scamper away from the port. Passing vegetable stalls and stopped chickens on bamboo poles, running in and out between all the legs of the humans, my head swims with all the different smells that tickle my nose. Fishy then meaty then smoky. I want to stop and investigate, but instead I run, run, run, rushing past men and women, wheels of carts, black cars, everything and everyone hurrying, shouting. Busy, busy, fast, fast.

We will get to where he wants us to be and what he wants to show me. A new, quiet place to play or hide, or where lots of brown legs and white legs sit down and eat. The smell makes me very hungry. Sometimes an owner will see us and throw us some food. Once or twice we try other places like that, but we just get chased out. My tail has been caught under a broom before now and, whenever it happens, I yelp and have to run even more fast.

4

Every so often some huge, stiff-looking birds fly low over the harbour but, even though they look like birds, I know they are called planes. They fly round and round and have what look like tails streaming out of the end of them. The tails look almost as long as mine. Whenever the planes appear, I flatten my ears right down because I know what is about to happen. A huge 'bang' from across the harbour followed by another and then another. Bang! Bang! The planes turn and swoop down even more low, or fall and rise again, like the birds high above me.

Sometimes a tail streaming from the back of a plane gets holes in and the banging stops, only for it to then start again. The planes never get hit though, just their big tails behind them, flapping in the wind. JoJo told me they do it so it doesn't all happen again, that it is just pretend, not for real like when he was small. When it is pretend there are huge bangs, but that is all. When it was real JoJo says he was more frightened than he has ever been. So, even though it is very noisy and a little bit scary, I am not frightened because I know it is just pretend. The most best thing about the pretend planes and the bangs though is that, whenever it happens, lots and lots of fish float up to the surface of the water.[1] JoJo told me it is because the fish are stunned. I don't know what he means by that. I think he means somewhere in between being asleep and stopping.

So that is why, even though I would like to fly, I don't think I would like to fly away. There are the ships and the boats, the sea and the sky, the birds and the fish, the humans... and JoJo of course. I love having a more big brother. He has black fur like me, but I have white paws as well and my tail is more long. Once we had a mother too. That's where we came from. I see pictures of her sometimes in my head, but I don't remember her. JoJo sometimes mentions her, but not very often.

He would rather tell me stories instead. Like when he was the same size as me now and it suddenly started to bang, bang, bang all the time. He said that men came from the big sea and all the humans who live here were scared. They used to hide or bang, bang back, but it was no use. More and more men came and JoJo had to hide as well. That's when he began to make mouses and rats stop moving and playing. So *he* could

---

[1] After World War II, British battalions stationed in Hong Kong used to fly drogues over the harbour for target practice. It has been documented that, when this happened, fish in the harbour were stunned by the echo and floated up to the surface.

carry on. The humans used to call it a Black Christmas.[2] It doesn't sound very nice to me. At all.

I am happy I am here now and not then. Back then JoJo did not have me, but now we both have each other. I don't know what I would have done. I still don't think I would have been able to do what he does with the mouses and the rats. And definitely not the snakes. Even JoJo runs away when they appear. When he makes me play away from the harbour you can see them sometimes, slithering along all slow; or when we run through the sloping grass you can see a long dark shape and if you get too close it will rise up and hiss. They have horrible little tongues and you have to run even more fast.

Every so often, near the sloping grass, men appear and run around and play with a ball. They have to run past each other and kick it into something. I don't really like it very much. All the humans running around scare me, but JoJo likes it a lot. Sometimes he runs over to where they are playing and tries to chase the ball. And sometimes, when we have a ball to play with, JoJo will find a box, tip it to one side and I have to stop him from getting the ball into the box. He is very clever. But often when I want to just lie in the box, JoJo pushes it over on me so I cannot get out. He is not very nice sometimes too.

Whenever we come down the hill and it is getting to dark time we pass a building with men and women going in. The smell of the women is more nice than the smell at the top of the grassy slope. The smell of the women makes my nose twitch and sometimes I even sneeze. They look very pink and pretty and they smile at me a lot.

They are always with men who look very stiff in their uniforms, but their buttons glint and shine and sometimes they smile at me too. Whenever lovely sounds come from inside there are always men and women moving around close together and it makes me want to wiggle my bottom a little bit.[3]

---

[2] The Japanese attacked Pearl Harbour and Hong Kong on 8th December, 1941. The battle of Hong Kong and subsequent surrender became known as Black Christmas.

[3] The HMS Tamar was the Royal Navy's shore base from 1897 to 1997. There was also a NAAFI (Navy, Army and Air Force Institute) on Stonecutters Island - an organisation created by the British Government in 1921 to provide recreational facilities including launderettes, shops, cafés, bars and clubs on British military bases and canteens on board Royal Navy ships. Simon saw the army, navy and NAAFI personnel dancing and wanted to join in.

We don't play round there very often though. There is a mean grey me with one green eye who hisses and chases us away whenever we see him. He is called Chairman and he is horrible. Even JoJo is scared of him. The last time we saw Chairman he came right up close to us and spat, 'This place is mine. I live here. If I ever see you here again then a very bad thing will happen to you… ' I don't know why he doesn't like us when we could all play together, but JoJo says he is nasty which means he is very bad and naughty.

Not every me who lives round here is horrible though. Sometimes I see a very pretty me called Lilette running around and playing. She is all white, has one big blue and one big gold eye and I like her a lot. I like her face, her fur, but most of all I like her scent. We don't play together though. I just see her and smile and she smiles back. JoJo tells me I should not be so shy and just say hello. I did say hello to her once, but she didn't say anything which made me feel very small and silly so I just gave up.

One more thing. There are lots of smalls too who always laugh and play with us but, when they catch me and JoJo, they only stroke us, they don't throw water or anything. It can be very busy and noisy and smelly here but, ever since I was a very small me, it has been fun to learn about which smells and noises are good and which are bad. It is busy because there are many humans here. They are all different shapes and smells and even colours sometimes. Some of them talk fast. Some of them use different words for the same things. But by watching and listening and thinking - and by JoJo helping me of course - more and more things make sense to me as I get more big and more big. So yes, I like it here because of all those things. Apart from Chairman and some of the humans that chase me sometimes, I know there is more good than bad.

2/ Coming and going

I feel some claws digging into my back and I turn around. It isn't JoJo though. It is Uboat, my friend. Uboat appears sometimes then disappears and comes back again. He likes to jump on board the ships that come into the harbour and go away on them. He said he used to live on a ship called HMS Snowflake, but he got into trouble on it, so when it stopped at a place far away called Newfoundland he jumped onto another ship and came here and that's when he met me.[4]

I smile when I see him and my whiskers twitch. They always do that when I am happy. We rub noses. He smells of salty water and his fur is sticky.

'Where've you been?'

'Where haven't I been?' He half chuckles, half purrs and jumps onto my back. 'I've been watching the seagulls on the sea and running up and down on a big boat. It's been fun, fun, fun!'

'And what else? What else have you seen?' I like Uboat's adventures almost as much as I like JoJo's stories. He has told me about places where everyone and everything belongs to a king. Of Captains on

---

[4] HMS Snowflake was a Royal Navy 'flower' class corvette on Atlantic convoy duties in World War II. In 1943 it picked up 62 survivors from the tanker British Ardour that was torpedoed and sunk by a German U-boat. There was a cat on board the HMS Snowflake called Uboat. It has been documented that, normally, he was a very clean cat, but the Captain ordered him off at Newfoundland for Uboat doing his business on the Captain's wardroom chair. For the purposes of this story, Uboat managed to hitch a lift on a ship, or ships, that eventually docked in Hong Kong.

ships, whales in the sea and dogs on the land. About tigers which are like big me's[5] and creatures called monkeys.

'Too many things to tell you. This time I have seen green birds that talk back to you. I have played on lots of sand next to the sea and burnt my paws. Once, when the ship landed somewhere, I jumped off and got chased by lots of little humans. They said they had never seen anything like me before. They just wanted to play and give me lots of nice food. It was fun, fun, fun!'

Uboat rolls on his back and waves his legs in the air before springing to his feet again. 'And what about you, what have you been doing?' he asks me.

'I have been playing in the alley and running in between legs and watching the birds,' I say, sitting up and licking a paw.

'Always watching, aren't you? Watching, watching. Have you ever been on the front of a ship and felt the sea water splash in your face?'

'No. You know I haven't.'

'Have you ever smelt something funny, turned your nose up at it and licked it and it was good, good, good?'

'Sometimes.'

'Have you ever woken up and not known where you are?'

'No. I always know where I am.'

'I know you do,' Uboat laughs. 'But can you remember what this place is even called?'

'Of course I can,' I say, trying to remember. I know Uboat told me once. 'It's called Ding Dong.'

Uboat lets out another loud laugh. 'Ha, ha. It's called Hong Kong, not Ding Dong. And this part is called Stonecutters Island.'

I feel very silly, but pretend not to be.

'Well, what does it matter what places are called as long as you like living where you are?'

'I don't know. It seems to matter to humans though.'

'Why?'

---

[5] Punctuational licence has been taken with the pluralising of the word 'me', using 'me's' throughout as the correct spelling – 'mes' – looks like a strange typo.

'Because if you know where you are from then you also know where you are not from. They like to know these things,' he continues, nodding at three pairs of human legs as they rush past us more quick.

'But why?'

'Because then you can protect the place where you are from.'

'Protect it from what?' I ask, confused.

'Others who are not from there, I suppose.' Uboat answers.

From. Not from. Now my head is spinning. What's wrong with wanting to go to a place and play in it if it's nice? Uboat is not from here, but that doesn't mean I don't like it when he jumps off his ship and comes to find me. That's why I don't like Chairman. All JoJo and me want to do is to play and to run around near the sloping grass, but Chairman doesn't like us doing that.

I look at Uboat.

'So, how long are you in this place for?' I ask him. 'On Stormcutters Island?'

'Stonecutters not Stormcutters,' Uboat laughs. 'I heard the men on the ship say we've docked to collect some stores and then we'll be going again.'

'Where are you going to this time?' I want to know.

'Who knows? Who knows?' Uboat pounces onto my tail. 'Somewhere with lots of exciting new smells and places to explore.'

'Don't you ever get scared you might get wet when you are on a ship?' My left ear twitches.

'I do get wet sometimes,' he laughs. 'But it's all part of the fun. You get used to it.'

A quick shiver runs through my little body at the very thought and all the way down to my tail that Uboat is now playfully pulling with his teeth.

'What about if you go to a place and humans don't want you to be there?'

'Oh, I don't know,' Uboat replies. 'That's for the humans to work out. Not me. Come on,' he squeals, springing up and away from me. 'Let's run.'

'Where to?' I ask him. It is still baking hot on my fur and I want to carry on lying here and look at the boats and the ships, at the birds and at all the humans hurrying around. They might even give me something to eat.

11

'Wherever our paws take us,' he chuckles and dashes off, through the port and up some steps. 'Come on, come on, come on!'

And so I follow him. He points out his ship, blue and white and huge. We run up steps, past some baskets, over a junk out of the water and rotting, in between lots of pairs of legs and into the alley. It is more cool here and a little bit more dark. The high, high buildings on either side seem to close me in. I look up and see a woman hanging out of her window, shaking a white sheet. Some drops of water splash onto my head and one splashes on my nose. I try to lick it and look up again to see Uboat's legs darting in and out between tables. There are some large green vegetables spilled out on the floor and he jumps on one, turns around and looks back at me.

I catch up with him.

'I have seen these being pulled out of the ground.'

'Where?' I want to know.

'I think it was called America,' he answers and skips away again. 'I like America.'

We come to the corner. There are chickens in baskets all piled high. Some of them are talking. Some of them are sitting down. Some have their backs to the door of the cage. All of them look unhappy.

'Poor chickens,' I say to Uboat.

'Yes,' he twitches his nose. 'They'll never know what it's like to be free, free, free on the open sea, sea, sea.' He looks sad. 'They do taste nice though.' And then he laughs.

'Uboat!' I don't like the thought of things moving around and then stopping. Even though they do taste nice.

We scamper round the corner and go down a maze of narrow alleyways, twisting and turning. I struggle to keep up with Uboat. He is more strong than me. He can run and run and run. I have to stop sometimes and have a rest. We see lots of women and smalls going into doorways in the alleys. Some of the women are crouched on the doorsteps washing vegetables in little bowls and slicing them. Some of them are cooking outside; big pots on stoves. There are yummy smells coming from all around and steam from the pots and from the doorways.

'Uboat,' I call to him and he stops and turns round.

'Yes?' He comes running back to me.

'I'm hungry.'

'So, what shall we do? Where shall we go?' He sniffles a little.

'Maybe if we just stay here they will throw us some food,' I reply, looking over at one of the women sitting on her doorstep.

12

She looks over at us both and hisses, 'Shweh, shweh.' She grabs a broom.

'I don't think so,' Uboat responds. 'She has a big, red, angry face. Look.'

I do and he is right. I know when humans do that it means they don't like us. She stands up to shoo us away so Uboat runs round and past her legs and I shoot right past her. We turn around a corner and run in between some crates before the alley opens out into a dusty road.

Uboat sniffs the air. A black car passes us on the road.

'Let's cross,' he squeals.

We get to the other side, run through a spiky bush and some pretty flowers, which make me sneeze again, until we find ourselves on a patch of yellowing grass.

Uboat sniffs.

'What's that smell?' he asks.

'It happens sometimes when there has been banging up there.' I nod over to where the grass is sloping upwards. I know which way the port is from here, which must mean... Suddenly, a grey me comes running towards us, getting more big and more big. A green eye catches the sun and it glints. It is big, bad, scary Chairman. My back legs wobble, my ears go flat and I have to sit down.

Chairman comes right up to us both and spits and hisses. 'What have I said? What have I said?' he hisses at us. '*I* live here. This is *my* place. Go away.' Uboat squares up to him. His back is arched and his tail is standing straight out.

'And what happens if we don't go away?' Uboat has made himself look very mean and he sounds different. 'Do you know who I am?'

Chairman looks at him. 'No. I have never seen you before.'

They begin to circle around each other, slow, slow.

'I am the king of where I am from. I am looking for a new place to live. And if I decide to live here I will bring hundreds and hundreds of my kind with me and you will be our first prisoner. Our first enemy.'

I don't really understand what Uboat is saying, but it all sounds a bit scary.

Chairman gives another little hiss, but eventually he turns around and slinks off.

We trot across the road, see some crates and hide behind one of them. Even though we are both shaking we are both laughing too.

'That was very brave of you,' I say to him. 'Pretending you were a king.'

Then, from behind another crate, a small grey me shoots out, runs across the road and dashes up the grassy slope.

'Oh no,' I mewl. 'Let's get out of here.'

We make our way more quick back to the port, darting through alleyways and running around and over boxes. A nice lady throws us some food, but we don't even stop to have a nibble. We get back to one of my best hiding places, right at the end of the harbour. The birds have flown away; they have been replaced by clouds. Twinkling lights are starting to appear from the buildings dotted around and from the big ships and other boats gently rising and falling, bobbing on the more dark water.

Uboat and I cuddle up together.

'I have to go soon,' Uboat nuzzles me.

I mew sadly.

'Why don't you come with me?' he asks.

I shake my head. 'I like it here. There's JoJo and there's— '

'Food?' Uboat laughs. 'There's food in other places. Lots of it.'

'No. I like listening to your adventures, but I don't think I'm ready to have an adventure of my own just yet. I'm not big enough.'

'When is big enough?' Uboat smiles, his whiskers twitching. We both close our eyes. I see birds flying in the sky and JoJo playing with a big fish and I see my mother. Not that I remember her. She's pretend. But here and now she is big and black and white and warm. It makes me feel nice and I think I purr.

A deep blast of a ship's horn wakens us from our little snooze. We are still curled up together.

'I know that sound.' Uboat glances at me. 'I have to go.'

He stands up, puts his front legs forward and stretches them. His tail swishes past my nose, tickling me.

'Until next time. Enjoy all your fish.'

And he scampers off into the dark. I can see him getting less and less big, even more well than I could if it was bright. I know I will see him again though. I always do.

I don't know whether to move or to stay here. I think I may go and find some more food in a bit. For the moment, I will stay curled up. Under here. Uboat can have his adventures. Watching the humans coming and going is adventure enough for me. I close my eyes and my mum appears again. She is smiling, smiling. She licks my nose, her big eyes right up close to mine. I am surrounded by her black and white fur, but then her fur seems to change. It turns into prickles, like the bush near the grassy slope where Chairman doesn't like us to play. There's no white in her fur now. It is getting more dark and more dark and more dark.

I sense a powerful smell. It changes from one I think I know to a scent I don't. I twitch my nose and open my eyes. I can see a shape moving towards me, all slow. Its back is humped and it is dragging itself more close, familiar yet also strange. The smell is surrounding me. I don't like it. I hear a whimper, almost as if it is coming from far away and I recognise it immediately.

'JoJo,' I call out and sit up. The shape twitches and slows down. I run over. It *is* him.

'JoJo, JoJo,' I cry out, nudging his face, nibbling his ear. His other ear is ragged and sticky. He is sticky all over. 'What's happened? What's happened?'

JoJo looks up at me. He can barely move. One of his back legs is twisted. He coughs and some dark, sticky liquid trickles out of his mouth. The smell is getting even more bad. It smells like he is disappearing into himself, away from me. I lick his face, but he closes his eyes.

'You've been playing in the alley with Uboat, haven't you?' He coughs again.

'Yes.'

'I smelt you. Then I went to the bad place. I was looking for you.' He opens his eyes. 'Chairman.'

'Chairman did this to you?'

'Yes. He came from nowhere. He jumped on me and scratched me everywhere. He attacked me all the way down the hill. I did this... ' JoJo tries to turn to look at his back leg and sighs again.

'Oh, JoJo, JoJo,' I squeal.

'He said this is for your friend the king... '

I close my eyes when JoJo mutters that.

'I have been crawling and crawling. I smelt you here. It hurts,' he whimpers.

'Where?' I rub his nose again.

'Everywhere. I have to... You need to— '

And then JoJo closes his eyes again. And he stops.

This does not make sense. This does *not* make sense. I push him with my nose. I lick his face, ignoring the sticky stuff. I even jump on his back and dig my claws in. But it's no use. He's stopped, he's stopped, he's stopped.

I stand up and let out a huge 'Yaaarwwl!' And another and another. Somewhere a human shouts. I arch my back. My tail is sticking straight out, stiff, like from behind the back of one of the planes with the bang, bang, bangs. I jump up and dash behind a box and out again. JoJo is still lying there, stopped.

I don't know what to do, so I run. I run and run and run, through the port, round a corner, turn around and back again. I run behind a box before poking my head out and looking around. I can see the ship Uboat is on edging out of the harbour. Uboat going. JoJo stopped. There are many lights everywhere, twinkling. Why are they twinkling? What is there to light up now? I cough and cough and a little ball of my dark fur comes up. And then I curl up more tight and I am screeching. I want to escape from all this real. From myself. I don't know what else to do. If I carry on screeching maybe everything will stop. Maybe I will stop too.

And then I start to shake. Even though I am hidden behind this box I do not feel safe. What if Chairman comes to find me too? I am all alone. No one is here to protect me. My legs are shaking, I am shivering all over. I feel so cold. What shall I do now? Where shall I go? I crouch behind the box and try to think of a picture, something that might make me jump up and run, to feel warm, to feel comforted. But nothing comes. I have nowhere to run and no one to run to. I lie there all still, scary pictures coming in and out of my head. Breathing fast, my nose and whiskers twitching. I cannot escape. I lie and wait, but for what, I don't know. All I can see are scary pictures and all I can feel is fear. Of being alone. JoJo has gone. I have no one. I lie there, I tremble and I wait.

Then I feel my tail sticking straight out behind me, all stiff. I try to curl it around me, but it won't move. I stretch my front paws, I twitch my ears, but I cannot move my tail. I am frozen. I am cold. I cannot move. I do not like this at all. What is happening to me? What is going to happen to me? I close my eyes. Maybe when I open them I will not be here? Maybe when I open them I will see JoJo? Maybe... What was that? I hear a noise behind me. I am too scared to move. There is something behind me. Chairman. He's here. He's found me. He is going to make me stop too. This is it.

I feel my tail being pulled. I am too scared to make any sound. I stretch my claws out in front of me to try to grab onto the ground, but it is no use. Pulling, pulling, I wait for the hiss and the claws to dig into my back. I don't like this. I want it to be bright and to see the birds. Not dark, I don't want to be here. Here they come now, the claws, I can feel them.

But they are not claws. I am being squeezed, but only a little. I open my eyes and turn my head. A human is looking at me. He is smiling and his eyes are a little wet and then I feel that his hands are warm.

'Hello, little fella,' he says to me. 'I thought there was something hiding. Your tail was sticking out. Come here, you're all shaking.' And he lifts me up and puts me in his arms. Who is he? What is he going to do to me?

'My, your heart is pounding,' he continues. He makes me feel all nice and warm. I stop shivering, my back legs dangle down.

'If I put you down, will you run away?' he asks me.

He makes to put me on the ground, but I quite like being in his arms. He must be able to tell that I don't want him to let me go because he stands straight up again and gives me another squeeze. I like being snuggled against his thick coat, all warm. This must be what having a mother is like.

'There, there,' he says. 'Do you want to come with me?'

Maybe I should struggle? Then he would put me down and I could run away. But where would I go? Who would I run to now? I feel safe. I feel protected.

'You sure you don't want me to let you go?'

I bury my head even more deep into his arm.

'OK,' he says. 'That settles it,' and before I know it we are walking away from the place where I live and where I am from, away from the alley, right round the harbour. Walking, walking, fast, fast in his arms. He is walking so quick and I feel so high up off the ground I feel like I am flying, like the birds up in the bright, bright sky. I am flying, flying, away, away…

3/ Now is all we have

I peer through a gap between the man's coat and his arm. I can see the dark water as we reach the huge, huge hulk of a ship. We pass by and keep walking until we reach another one. He stops and I can see him looking up. There is something with rails on either side resting on the dock, leading upwards. It looks like a big tongue ready to lick us both up. We step onto it and walk up, wobbling a bit until we come to a rest on the ship.

'Don't make a sound now,' he whispers to me. 'I'll probably get the skipper's table for this.'[6] He doesn't need to tell me to be quiet. I am too confused and shaking too much to make any sort of sound. I peep out from under the man's arm. I see a railing running down the side of the ship and some little round windows. Then I spy some men standing near the top of the tongue and I shrink right back. He puts his hand on top of my head and pushes me back against him even more.

'Sshh,' he says, even more quiet. 'That's Sharpe, the quartermaster and Welburn, the bosun's mate. If they catch us I'm done for.'

We must creep past them because I can feel him moving and then hear him say, 'OK,' and he taps me on my head through his coat. I peep out, just a little bit. It smells strange. The ship has a different smell to anything I have smelt before. I'm not sure what. It is a mixture of humans and other smells and one very similar to the scent of the bad place. The

---

[6] To get put on a charge.

place where… I squeeze my eyes tight shut so the pictures of bad things go away.

We creep along, passing the railings on one side and the little round windows on the other. I want to look over the railing to see how far down the sea is, but I am trapped in between the man's arm and his body. I try to look up to see if I can see a mast or a flag like JoJo told me about, but I can't. I am too buried underneath coats and arms.

JoJo, JoJo. What if he hadn't really stopped? Maybe he might have moved after I'd run away? Maybe he was just sleeping? Or stunned? But I don't think he would have opened his eyes. He was covered in all the dark, sticky stuff and he smelt different and he seemed as if he wasn't there anymore. If I had stayed it would have been just me left all on my own, but now I am here with this man and, even though I have never been on a ship before, Uboat says they are fun. It doesn't really feel much like fun right now, but it doesn't feel too scary either. It seems like this man wants to look after me. I blink slow. I would rather be close to this strange man than be anywhere near horrible Chairman.

We duck under a chain and underneath some stairs. We go through an open door and step inside the ship itself. It is more hot now and it smells of humans even more. We get underneath what looks like a hiding place. He grabs a big fishing net hanging from a hook, attaches it to another hook and, with great difficulty, manages to clamber inside it. It swings from side to side as we get in. He gets a blanket, places it over himself and sits me on top of it.

I look at him properly now and he looks right back at me. Not quite a man, he looks more like some of the smalls that chase me and… that used to chase me and… I try to make the pictures go out of my head and so look at all the pictures of pretty ladies that are in his hiding place instead. They must be very cold without their clothes though.

He smiles again. 'My name's George.[7] I wonder what we shall call you.' I can smell his breath. It makes me feel a bit sick. His eyebrows move close together. 'I think I'll call you Simon. Do you like being on a ship, Simon?'

---

[7] Reports are varied as to who took Simon on board in April 1948 – Captain Ian Griffiths or Ordinary Seaman George Hickinbottom. Hickinbottom left Amethyst a few months later and Simon was also befriended by Petty Officer George Griffiths. For narrative purposes, a sailor called 'George' has been created but any resemblance to real persons, living or dead, is purely coincidental.

Simon?! I ask myself. Simon?! JoJo used to call me Titch. I yowl and my whiskers droop. Thinking about JoJo makes me sad. Perhaps being called Simon will make my whiskers twitch and make me want to run around again? I hope so.

I look around. I am still trying to get used to all the different smells. It smells stale. It smells damp. And it is still hot. Almost as hot as when I was birdwatching and daydreaming and Uboat came along and jumped on my back. I can see now there are lots of other men in this place too. Like George, they are lying back and swinging a little in tiny beds hanging up. Some of them are making snuffling, growling noises. It is quite dark, but it just means I can see more. I can see a table and some chairs, and pipes running across the roof and lots of other things I don't recognise. I wonder if this is like the inside of the ships Uboat has lived on.

George sits up a little and manages to take his boots and trousers off. He wraps his boots in his trousers, places them behind his head and lies back again. I am not quite sure what to do. My pictures in my head are all jumbled up. I feel a little bit scared, a little bit sad, but a little bit something else as well. Something tells me the best thing for me to do is just to stay here with George so I move round and round ready to settle on him. I look at his feet. They are very dirty and smelly. George makes a little noise, lifts me up and turns me round so I am facing him.

'Sorry, Simon,' he smiles. 'Your tail was tickling my nose.'

And that reminds me of Uboat again, just before he ran off and left me. I make a promise to myself - and to JoJo: I will *really* try to be brave from now on. Just like Uboat is and JoJo was. Uboat said living on ships and going to different places is fun, but I think he says those things because he does not get scared like me. So, I will try to be like him. To be like both of them.

I notice George's eyes are starting to close, but I want to be awake more than I want to go to sleep. Maybe I should just lie here. He said I should not make a sound so, yes, I will just lie here and look around and be quiet; a little bit scared, a little bit sad, a little bit something else…

I listen to the other men making noises. George starts to make them too. He seems to be talking in between his snuffles. How funny. I wonder who he is talking to and if he has pictures in his head like I do.

As I close my eyes, I hear another noise. It is a 'clack, clack' sound and I can hear some panting too. My eyes dart around, my ears flatten right back and my whiskers go all aquiver. I can smell something as well. Suddenly, a large, furry head appears in the hiding place and stares right at me. Oh no! It is the head of a dog. Some of the dogs that run around the harbour want to chase me and eat me up, but some of the others are quite friendly. I wonder if this one is a friend or… not a friend. I don't quite know what to do. I think of both JoJo and Uboat being brave so I decide to do that. Or at least pretend.

The dog keeps on looking at me. But it hasn't growled or shown me its teeth.

I give a little cough. 'You're a dog,' I say to the furry head, finally.

'Yes, I am,' the dog answers. 'Able Seadog Peggy at your service.'[8] And she licks my face. 'Who are you?'

'I think I'm called Simon,' I reply.

'You only *think* you're called Simon? How frightfully queer,' Peggy responds. 'What are you doing on here?'

'I'm not sure. I was with… and then I was hiding and then... ' I start to whimper.

Peggy puts her wet nose right up to my face. I shrink back a little.

'Don't worry,' she mutters. 'I won't bite you. Not all dogs are grumpy, you know.'

I feel a bit less bad now. I don't want any more bad to happen. Funny how this dog seems to be good yet Chairman, another me, is not.

'Would you care for me to show you around?' she asks.

'I think I would like that very much. But I think George here wants me to stay put.'

'You think an awful lot,' Peggy snorts. 'I'm more of a, how you would say, a doer myself. I'll wager George here is asleep judging by his snoring, so I vote we go.'

Snoring. What a funny word.

I stand up, which makes the bed wobble and swing even more, and spring onto the floor.

'This way,' says Peggy and I can feel her hot breath on me. It smells even more bad than George's. Or the stale smell of feet in here. She heads off and so I follow her. She has a brown head, a brown and white body and a brown tail. Her bottom wobbles as she pads off. In fact she is quite wobbly all over. She must eat a lot of food on this ship. Maybe it won't be so bad after all.

'Is it always so hot here?' I ask her bottom.

---

[8] Peggy was the ship's dog.

'Oh yes,' she replies. 'Except when we're out at sea. Sometimes it's even hotter. You get used to it though.'

As Peggy squeezes through the gap underneath the stairs and I rush through, I notice both Peggy's paws and mine are making that 'clack, clack' sound. We are back outside on the ship's deck. The twinkling stars and the cool breeze are quite nice though, so I decide to lick myself and give myself a quick clean. Peggy barks, making me spring right to my feet and almost fall over.

'Don't jump over the gunwale,' Peggy gives a little laugh.

'What's a gunwale?'

'The sides of the ship. If you go overboard then I wager I would have to jump over too and fish you out and I would really rather not do that, thank you very much.' Peggy's tail droops a little.

'Don't you like water either?' I ask.

'Gosh, I love water. It's just that I've had a most wonderful brush this evening. Haven't you noticed my frightfully glossy coat?'

Peggy trots off again. 'Come on. Let me take you to the bow.'

She sets off, panting a little and so I follow; the little round windows to my left, the - what I now know to be the gunwale - and the sea below to my right. There are many things to jump over, under and through. With my whiskers I can judge the gaps and do it very easily, but Peggy has to push herself through. The gaps are not very small really, but I suppose it is more hard if you are big. Although Peggy starts to trot off ahead of me, I catch up with her with ease. I can't get past her though and so my head ends right up close to her tail and bottom. As she tries to squeeze through a gap, struggling under the strain, she lifts up her tail and gives a little parp. The smell is even more bad than the one from the feet of all the sleeping men in that room.

Peggy turns round. 'I do apologise,' she whispers. 'I do that sometimes.'

My nose wrinkles.

Peggy composes herself. 'This side of the ship is called the starboard side,' she explains. 'And those boats up there are lifeboats.'

Are boats alive? I didn't think they were.

'And those rings there,' she nods. 'Well, if the men throw them into the water or drop the boats in, it means... well it means an awfully terrible thing has happened probably.'

'What do the rings do?' I ask, puzzled.

'They rescue people,' she answers. 'It means they save lives.'

Just like George saved mine, I think.

We reach some more stairs and start to climb up them. 'And the other side of the ship is called the port,' Peggy continues.

She huffs and puffs as we climb up the steep stairs. I jump from step to step and get to the top much more quick than she does. Finally she reaches me. 'And this is called the gun deck.'

Star. Gunboard. Portdeck. So many new words. Uboat never said about any of these things when he was telling me his stories. I look around.

'What are those two long noses?' I ask Peggy.

'Those are called turrets.' She goes up to them and gives them a little sniff. 'They're used to shoot things. They make a terribly deafening sound.'

I give them a little sniff too. 'What does 'shoot' mean?' I ask her. I shoot past things when I run, but I know I don't make a deafening noise.

'So many questions, Simon. Hopefully you'll never need to know what shoot means. Come on.'

We run across the gun deck and get to the very front of the ship. I am back near the tongue again, but I cannot see or smell the bosun master or the quarter mate.

'This is the bow,' Peggy says proudly yet panting. We are standing next to some more turrets. I look out. I can see another huge ship just in front and the harbour stretching out to the big sea, all lit up by stars and the lights of the buildings dotted around. I try to picture me going out to sea, the cool wind pushing my ears back and with all sorts of birds flying overhead.

I turn around. 'What's that?'

'That's the flag deck up there and that's the bridge,' Peggy explains, looking all serious now, just like when JoJo tells me - used to tell me - not to gobble up too much food.

'That's not a bridge,' I chuckle. 'I know what bridges are. You run up and down them over water and roads.'

'This is the bridge on a ship, dear Simon,' Peggy replies, sounding a bit haughty. Haughty. That was one of JoJo's most best words. 'It's where the Captain sits and some of the others work and make the ship turn. Honest to goodness... '

So, just like when different humans have different names for the same thing, I think to myself. Sometimes there is the same name for different things. My head spins some more.

'I'm not allowed in there very often,' Peggy continues. 'So I wager that you won't be allowed in there either. And just behind the

24

bridge is the cabin where the Captain sleeps. So don't even *think* about going in there.' Captain. Now I've heard of that word.

As she says that, a man emerges from behind the bridge and walks towards us. He is dressed in white, holding a drink and has fog coming out of his mouth. Scary. Me and Peggy both shrink down against the turret.

'Quick,' mutters Peggy. 'That's him now. It would be awfully bad form if he saw us. Well - you.'

I shiver and make a run for the stairs. So this is the Captain, and one who has fog coming from his mouth as well. I am relieved to hear Peggy following behind. Fast, fast, fast I go before finding a place to hide. Hot breath and panting, Peggy eventually catches up with me. I can see her tummy going in and out, in and out.

'My, my, Simon,' she exclaims, her tongue lolling around. 'You are remarkably speedy, aren't you?'

'Do you think he saw us?' I ask, my eyes gleaming and wide with fear.

'I don't think so. He didn't shout after us, did he?' Peggy tries to squeeze into my hiding place, but can't quite manage it. She gets her breath back.

'Oh lord,' she suddenly gives a little laugh. 'I've just realised what you are.'

I thought she knew what I was? I look at her, confused.

'You're a stowaway.'

'A what-away?'

'Someone who sneaks on board a ship.'

Hmm. I'm not sure I like the sound of that. But I didn't sneak on. I was brought on. By George. I look at the floor. Peggy sees me looking sad.

'Oh, don't worry,' she tries to comfort me. 'It will be all right. You'll see. Everything is better in the cold light of day.'

We both sit in silence. My nose wrinkles.

'Was that you again?' I ask.

Peggy looks at the floor.

'It must have been those biscuits I ate before.'

She stands up.

'Come on, let's get you back to George.'

I spring to my feet. Peggy pushes herself up.

'Now, can you remember where it is?'

I find my way back without trouble. Guided by smells. I'm good with smells. Away from one and into another, equally as bad.

We stand outside the dark room where the men are sleeping.

'So. Welcome to the HMS Amethyst, little Simon stowaway.[9] Do you like it?'

'I think it is a bit smelly but, yes, I think I like it. I wonder if I will be allowed to stay. What do you think?'

'I've told you, silly Simon, I don't really spend too much time bothering with all of that thinking nonsense. Yesterday is old, tomorrow is brand new and now is all we have. Do not worry.'

And, with that, Peggy trots off somewhere, her belly swinging like the beds here in the smelly room. I scamper to where George is sleeping, jump onto a chair and back onto his chest. He doesn't move at all. I close my eyes and hope the only pictures I see are nice ones and not any bad, scary ones.

'Now is all we have, now is all we have.' I feel the comforting rise and fall of George's chest and purr myself to sleep.

---

[9] HMS Amethyst was a Modified Black Swan-class sloop of the Royal Navy. She was laid down by Alexander Stephen and Sons of Linthouse, Govan, Scotland on 25th March 1942, launched on 7th May 1943 and commissioned on 2nd November 1943. After World War II she was modified and redesignated as a frigate. At the time of this story, she was in Hong Kong.

4/ Cold and invisible

I open my eyes. I'm not quite sure where I am, but the smell of humans soon reminds me, followed by the sound of them coughing and spluttering awake. Some of them have colours and shapes on their arms. What are those? George is still fast asleep, his mouth wide open. As the other men stretch and get out of their swinging beds some of them spot me and call out.

'Hey, hey, what do we have here?' says one.

'I wonder if Peggy has seen this. I bet she'll eat it for breakfast,' another laughs. I'm only glad I met Peggy last night otherwise I would be really scared now.

Some of the men come over. One of them is long and thin with very red hair. Another has brown hair and the other one has no hair at all. I shrink back. I must have got my claws out too because George wakes up with an 'Oww!', banging his head as he does so.

'I see you've got yourself a little mate,' the one with no hair chuckles as he prods George. 'What were you thinking, that it'd make a good substitute for a lady?' and all the men roar. The sound of the men laughing all at once makes me jump. George rubs his head and his eyes.

'I think I had too much grog while ashore last night. I was trying to clear my head before I came back on board and I heard this little fella.' He tries to sit up, but he swings from side to side and lies back instead.

'Awww. Too much heart. That's you George,' the red hair man laughs.

'Aye. And not enough brains,' says the one with no hair. 'What d'you think Cap'n will say?'

'I don't quite know. I didn't really think.' George's eyebrows move close together.

What did Peggy say about me last night? That I think a lot. Not like her. And here is George saying the same thing. How funny.

'Well, you'd better come up with a plan pretty quick, ol' Georgie boy,' no hair man continues. 'He'll be wanting to speak with us in the mess soon.'

'Move out of the way now fellas,' George replies, finally managing to stand up. 'I need the washroom.'

Yes, he really does, I think.

'Mebbe that'll wash some sense into ya,' the man with brown hair calls out as George slinks off.

As I lift my paw up to give myself a morning wash too some of the men drift away whilst others sit there rolling paper and putting it in their mouths. They put some fire up to their mouths - why do they do that? - and blow fog out, just like the Captain last night. As I wash, I watch them and wonder why they would want to hurt themselves. Some of them are quite noisy and shout out to each other, but I don't feel as scared now, so long as they don't try to set fire to *my* face too. As I finish washing, I hear a familiar 'clack, clack, clack', turn around and see Peggy peering at me.

'Good morning.' Peggy's tail is wagging. 'I see you've met some of the sailors. Have they been joshing with you?'

'Here, Peggy, Peggy,' no hair man calls her over. He is sitting at a table and looks like he has a biscuit. Peggy trots over, her tail wagging even more. She jumps up and sits next to the man.

'And how about your little friend?' the man says to Peggy, rubbing her head. 'Well done for not taking a bite out of her. Here, Blackie, come over here.'[10]

Blackie? I thought I was called Simon? Maybe there's another me in here I haven't seen?

Peggy nods at me to join them, so I jump down from the swinging bed and pad over. No hair man pats his knee, so I spring up and land in his lap.

'Careful there, Gurns,' the dark haired man says. 'Don't be stealing George's girlfriend now.'

Blackie? Girlfriend? Humans really are so very strange.

---

[10] The crew called him both Simon *and* Blackie.

28

Gurns strokes me and I purr. My tail is flicking from side to side a little. The man with dark hair puts something in his mouth.

'Oh, give us a smoke, McCunnell,' Gurns asks.

'Give me some of your kye then and I'll think about it.'[11] McCunnell lights a paper thing in his mouth and fog comes out from it. He puts his face close to mine and breathes all the fog out right into my face. It makes my eyes sting. I'm not sure I like this McCunnell man very much.

'Get away with ya,' Gurns says and pushes McCunnell's arm away from me. I look over at Peggy, but she is too busy eating something to notice.

'Quick game of cards anyone?' asks the man with red hair.

'Not a chance, Ginger,' McCunnell replies. 'We need to be shipshape and Bristol fashion for oh seven hundred.'

Gurns reaches across the table and gets a large glass jug of water. Another man has appeared and he plops some things into the water. They clink as they all fall into the jug and some droplets splash onto me. I twitch.

'Oh, get all wet did ya?' McCunnell snorts. 'Can't see you enjoying yourself much on here then. Maybe we should throw you overboard. You'd soon get used to the water.'

Maybe he's right. I don't feel so safe now George isn't here and with Peggy having a new friend in food. What am I doing on here anyway? What did Peggy say I was? A stoneaway? And where am I from? Stonecutters Island? A stoneaway. Away from Stonecutters Island. Maybe I should just jump down off Gurns's knee and run to the stairs and through all the gaps and down the big tongue? But what if the big tongue isn't there? Would I be brave enough to jump over the gunwale and splash into the sea and swim, swim, swim?

Gurns has poured some of the water out from the jug into lots of glasses. The tinkles coming from inside the jug and a flash of light catch my eye. I look at the jug and at the things inside bobbing up and down. I can see right through them. I wonder what they are. I think Ginger sees me looking because he pushes the jug over to me. Gurns looks down at me and I peer up at him.

---

[11] Hot chocolate.

'Oh, sorry, Blackie. I bet you're thirsty aren't you? Fetch a dish, McCunnell.'

'Fetch it yourself,' he answers.

Gurns sighs and stands up. As he does so, I spring up from his knee and land on the table.

''Ere, get off,' McCunnell cries and makes to push me away.

'Leave him be,' Gurns glares at McCunnell, sitting back down. Even Peggy looks up and gives a little growl.

I look at the men, at Peggy and back at the men again. But I am more fascinated by the jug of water and the tinkling sound coming from inside. I creep over to it as if I am about to pounce on JoJo's tail. My back is lowered and my whiskers are twitching. I reach the jug and sniff it. It smells of cold. I lift myself up on my back legs, rest my paws onto the jug and look down into it. I can hear something, but I cannot really see anything. Then, oh heavens, what am I doing? I reach down with my paw into the water. It is really cold and it really tickles, but it is only like when I pull a stunned fish from out of the water outside.

I bat my paw and can feel something. It makes a sound against the side of the jug. I twist my paw around and fish out the cold thing I can feel and hear, but cannot really see. It plops from out of my paw and lands onto the table, slithering a little as it does so.

All the men explode with laughter. Apart from McCunnell. He just sits there, but Peggy gives a little bark and smiles at me.

'I think we've got ourselves a fisherman.' Gurns lifts me up and places me back on his knee.

George comes back in, all dressed and smelling nice.

'Have I missed something?'

'Not 'arf.' Ginger laughs. 'Think we've got ourselves an entertainer. Do it again,' he says to me.

So, more for George's benefit than anything, I put my paw back into the water again and scoop out a... whatever it is.[12]

Gurns rubs my head. 'Well done, Blackie,' he smiles, his eyes shining.

---

[12] It has been documented that one of Simon's favourite tricks was to fish ice cubes out of jugs of water.

30

'Simon, not Blackie,' George corrects Gurns. 'His name is Simon.'

I jump down from the table. That's right. My name is Simon.

I feel a lot less bad now.

Peggy comes over to me. 'Don't worry,' she licks my face. 'I would have jumped over to rescue you if mean McCunnell had thrown you overboard.'

And that makes me feel even more good.

'Come on,' she mutters, and clack, clacks out.

We run through the sleeping room and back out to where the stairs are.

'This way,' Peggy half trots, half waddles.

We duck in between the thick, thick chain and another turret until we get right to the back of the boat. We dart - well, I dart, Peggy pushes herself - through many pairs of legs in white flappy trousers all walking fast and running up stairs, busy, busy. Some of the sailors notice Peggy and give her a quick pat on the head, but they don't say anything to me. Maybe they don't see me. Peggy is a lot more big than me so maybe I am hidden. Or perhaps humans only see what they want to see and not what they don't.

'This is the stern,' Peggy explains. 'When we are out at sea, sometimes I sit here and watch the white frothy water path we leave behind us. It's awfully good fun. It's also where I do, you know... '

She looks down.

'Where you do what?' I ask her, cocking my head.

'You know, my um... ' Peggy puts her head right up to mine. 'My business,' and she makes a little squatting motion.

'I'll wager back home you just go wherever you like?' she continues.

She's right; I did go wherever I wanted. Even the places I got chased away from.

'Well, on here you need to be much more considerate where you go about doing your, er, business,' she gives a little cough. 'Otherwise you get into the most awful trouble.'

I nod. But I still don't know what she means by condiderate business. It sounds very posh. A bit like Peggy.

Peggy composes herself. 'Anyway, let's continue with the tour.'

We run up some steps leading to the middle of the boat.

'This part is called the quarterdeck,' Peggy tells me. There are lots of sailors all working hard, scrubbing and cleaning. They look very nice in white. The sun is shining down as they work. We scamper down the steps and back to the stern.

'This way. I want to show you one of my favourite places.'

We come to a space full of boxes and lots of other things. It makes me want to explore.

'This is the stowage,' Peggy explains. 'It's where the sailors stow all their equipment and everything they need. I curl up and sleep in here sometimes.' She clambers into a slightly battered box. There is a large, chewed stick inside it. 'That's where I was before I smelt you last night.'

We both sniff around before we pad out from the stowage and back to the smelly place where the men are.

'Let's run through it quickly,' she suggests.

'Does this place have a name as well?' I ask Peggy.

'Oh yes. I do apologise. This is the lower deck.'

As we run through, some of the men call out after us, 'Here Peggy, hey Simon,' but we do not stop. Instead we get to a place that is very hot indeed.

'This is the engine room. When the boat is out at sea all these parts move and it gets very smoky and it's frightfully noisy. I don't much like it here. Come on.'

We pass through more doorways until we come to a big room. A room that has lots and lots of tables in it. It smells totally different to anywhere else on the ship. The smells in this room are yummy. The thick flavoured air makes my mouth water.

'This is the mess deck where they eat their food,' Peggy tells me. Some sailors are sitting down as we pass through.

'What's that?' one of them calls out.

'Georgie-boy's new friend,' I hear another say.

'Oh, I've just realised. I bet you're most frightfully famished, aren't you?' Peggy asks me. 'Where are my manners? Let me take you to my most favourite place of all. It really is first rate.'

The yummy smell gets more strong and more strong as we scamper through what she tells me is a galley. It's only when Peggy nudges me with her nose and yaps at me to keep moving I realise I'm standing still with my nose in the air imagining the taste of those delicious smells. Next we run through a warm, steamy room which I learn is called a laundry room before we get to a locked door.

'That's called the ops room,' she explains 'But it isn't my favourite place. Just a bit further now. This is it.'

I look all around me, but can't see anything.

'Look up.' Peggy motions with a paw.

When I do so, I notice a large friendly face beaming back at us behind an opening.

'Hullo, Peggy,' the face says. 'My, my, what do we have here?'

I look at Peggy. Her tongue is hanging right out. 'This is the stores,' she drools. 'It's like a shop.' And she gives a large bark, her tail wagging.

The friendly face throws Peggy something and she starts to gobble it up. Hasn't she eaten already? The human taps his hand on the ledge. I suppose it is for me to jump up. I spring up and land on it perfectly.

'Hello, sailor,' the friendly face says. So am I a sailor now too? 'You're awfully pretty aren't you?'

I purr and rub my head against his hand, my tail sticking straight up. I like this man.

'I'm Pauloni. By name and by nature,' and he laughs to himself.[13] 'Let's see what we've got for you, shall we?'

He disappears for a second before coming back with a small tin. He opens it and it is full of little fish all packed inside, all stopped.

'Pilchards,' Pauloni says.

He scoops them out onto a plate and I eat them all up, yum, yum, yum. I am so hungry I have forgotten all about Peggy. I lick my lips and look down at her.

She is looking sad.

'None for me?' she barks.

'Oh, Peggy. Hey girl, good girl.' Pauloni beckons her over. She puts her front paws up to the ledge, licking his hand and wagging her tail as he strokes her, all thoughts of food soon forgotten.

We hear a piercing whistle coming from the mess deck. Peggy instantly jumps back down and sets off, her tail still wagging. What else can I do but follow her?

'Bye, sailors,' Pauloni calls after us.

We both run into the mess deck at the same time. There are lots of men there and one man, standing up. There is no fog coming from his mouth now, but I recognise him as the Captain. He turns round, sees Peggy and then he sees me.

His face drops.

---

[13] Pauloni often speaks polari, a language used by the navy and homosexuals, amongst others. Omi-paloni means gay man and palone means woman.

HMS Amethyst
Photo courtesy of the PDSA[14]

---

[14] **The** People's Dispensary for Sick Animals is a veterinary charity in the United Kingdom. It was founded in 1917 by Maria Dickin to provide care for the sick and injured animals of the poor.

5/ Two by two

I look at the floor. I don't know where to put myself or what to do. I feel like I am sinking, right down into this floor. Maybe I should run now, although if I splash into the sea Peggy would only come and get me anyway. Peggy. Maybe she can help me. I look at her.

'What shall I do?' I mewl as I give myself another clean.

She doesn't have time to answer because the Captain barks instead. 'Who is responsible for this?' He looks around and all the men who were muttering now go very quiet.

George stands up.

'Me, sir.'

'He was drinking, Captain,' a voice pipes up. It is McCunnell.

'Drinking?' the Captain snaps in a loud, scary voice. 'Drinking when on duty. Well, we can't have any of that. Who's ever heard of such a thing?'

George coughs and looks at the floor. 'I had some leave so I thought— '

'Thought what?' the Captain booms. 'That you would bring an illegal on board? Whatever next! Leave the thinking to me, lad.'

Peggy's tail is right between her legs now. I can smell something I know again.

The Captain is standing very straight. He looks very smart in his white uniform. His buttons are even more shiny than the ones I have seen before. He marches over to me and Peggy. I think he is going to pick me up. Instead he bends down in front of Peggy.

'What do you make of the situation, Peggy? Friend or foe?'

Peggy licks his hand and wags her tail a little. She comes over and lies down right next to me. She nuzzles my nose and rests a paw on my back. I let out a purr. The most best purr I have ever purred. I look up at the Captain. He is looking right back at me and Peggy. I let out another purr. The Captain smiles. I let out one more purr and close my eyes. I can feel my chest pounding, pounding, but Peggy is lying right next to me making me feel all warm. I half expect to be picked up and thrown – sploosh - right overboard. But nothing happens, so instead I open my eyes again, blinking as I do.

The Captain stands up, looks back at the sailors and points to me and Peggy.

'And there was I thinking their kind were mortal enemies. Perhaps there's a lesson for all of us.'

McCunnell snorts.

The Captain turns back to me. I give my best miaow.

'Well, well,' he says. 'It seems like we have another sailor on board,' and all of the men give a little laugh.

'I don't quite know why you're laughing,' the Captain addresses George. 'You're on deck duties for the next thirty days.'

'Aye, aye, sir,' George replies. His smile goes upside down.

'Bringing this on board. Whatever next?' the Captain continues. 'We'll make a sailor out of you yet.'

I realise my ears are flattened right down, so I spring them up again and walk slow over to the Captain. He bends down to stroke me.

'You remind me of my Monty back home,' he smiles.[15] 'A most beautiful creature. And what, pray, is your name?'

'I called him Simon, sir,' George pipes up.

'Ah, Simon. Well, welcome aboard HMS Amethyst. Now, I don't know if you are aware of this, but everyone on board this ship has a job to do. I am the Captain. And a damn fine one at that.'

All the men let out another laugh.

'Your friend, George, is a most excellent deck scrubber.' The men laugh some more.

---

[15] It has been documented that he had a cat called Monty back home with his wife and children.

'And your friend Peggy there... ' Peggy wags her tail at hearing her name. 'Well, Peggy can smell the enemy coming from one hundred paces.'

And I can smell her coming from two hundred, I think to myself.

'So, if you're going to stay on board the Amethyst, this fine specimen of a ship, you can jolly well look after her like everyone else. Now, what job shall I assign you?'

'How about he gets the bosun's punch?' one of the men calls out.[16]

'A few of the men have been coming down with the lurgy, Captain,' another calls out. 'We think it's because of the— '

'Ah, of course,' the Captain interrupts, beaming broadly. 'Our own blasted enemies on here. As of today Simon, I order you become our rat catcher with the rank of Ordinary Seaman Simon.'

Seaman Simon. I like the sound of that. Am I ordinary though? And chasing after rats sounds like fun. I wouldn't mind running around this ship and doing that.

'You see, we have a huge rat problem on board this ship. Reminds me of the Hun. They just keep coming and coming. So you... ' he looks right at me now, 'From now on it's *your* job to catch as many of the blighters as you can. And kill them.'

I'm not quite sure what he means by that although, for some reason, it sounds like a little less fun than just playing with and chasing them.

'Stop them in their tracks,' the Captain continues. 'And stop them eating all of our darned supplies.'

Stop them? I think I know what he means now. More than sleep and more than stun. He means to stop them like Chairman stopped...

I swallow hard, but a little bit of pilchard comes up. I don't much like the thought of stopping anything. Not at all. I don't much like the rats that live back where I am from, but that doesn't mean that I want to see them stopped.

Peggy must notice I have gone from sad to happy to sad again because she comes over. 'Fret not, dear Simon,' she mutters. 'We'll work something out.'

---

[16] An old navy joke in which a new recruit was told to go and ask for a 'bosun's punch', whereupon the bosun would usually hit him in the face.

We both lie down as the Captain goes over to join the rest of the men. He starts to speak to them, although I am not really listening. I am shaking too much and my fur is quivering all over.

'Right, men,' the Captain clears his throat. 'As you're all aware, operations begin again at oh eight hundred hours tomorrow. We have re-fuelled and stocked up on all our supplies and, apart from those damn rats... ' He looks over at me, '...we should have enough for our next mission. As a reward, those of you who have been on ops duty are allowed onshore this evening. Cinderella leave.'[17]

Some of the men give a little cheer.

'Providing that none of you come back with any animals of course.'

'Not even any lions?' one of them asks.

'Of course not any darned lions. What do you think this is - Noah's darned Ark?'

What's Noah's darned Ark?

The Captain carries on addressing the men. 'The rest of you can remain here. There's still a lot of work to do.'

'Permission to speak, sir?' A man who is balancing a line of hair on his lip puts his hand up.

'Granted,' he answers gruffly.

'What is our next mission? Or is it classified?'

'Intelligence in Malaya informs us there is bandit activity in Perak. So tomorrow we head to the Straits.'

'Aye, sir.' The man who is balancing the hair sits down.

'Patrol duties only,' the Captain continues. 'To protect British interests and to serve our king and country.'

'Our king and country,' the sailors all repeat together.

'Back to your stations,' the Captain commands.

The men all stand at the same time, raise their hands to touch the side of their heads, make a clicking noise with their shoes and file out. I've never seen so many humans doing the same thing at the same time before.

'That includes you two,' the Captain remarks, glancing at me and Peggy.

---

[17] Naval terminology for being back on board by midnight.

Peggy sits up and troops out. I follow close behind. As I do so I see McCunnell grab George by the arm.

'Seems like you got off lightly there,' McCunnell scowls.

George smiles back at McCunnell. 'Yes. It's a darned good job he's an animal lover, I'll say. Right, up to the deck for me.'

I pad off ahead of Peggy but, unsure of where to put myself, I end up slowing down and waiting for her.

'Well, I don't know about you, but I fear it may be snooze time for Peggy,' she yawns. 'It's all been awfully exciting so far, hasn't it?'

I am too awake to even think about wanting to close my eyes. Besides, my heart is still pounding about the job the Captain has given to me. We trot through the lower deck and reach the stow, stoneage, the place where Peggy likes to sleep. She settles herself on the floor and rests her head on a paw. I turn round and round, but I don't really want to lie down.

'Stop pacing around,' Peggy snorts. 'What's the matter?'

'I don't really think I want to do my job,' I mewl sadly.

'None of us want to work, Simon,' Peggy replies. 'But it's something we must all do you know. To serve king and country and all that.'

But I don't have a king. I know what they are and what they do and that they live in faraway places, but I know I don't have one. I don't belong to a king. I don't really belong to anyone.

'No,' I whisper. 'I mean I don't want to do that… thing with the rats.'

'Kill them, you mean?' Peggy laughs. 'Oh dear, dear, little Simon. What are you? A mouse? Honest to goodness.'

I know I'm not a mouse. I am a me. But a me who doesn't want to stop rats from doing just that.

'Do you like rats, Simon?' Peggy looks at me.

'I don't know. Where I live - where I used to live - I used to see them and they used to see me, but we would play away from each other.'

'There's good and bad in every one of us Simon… '

I'm not sure there is any bad in me. And definitely not in JoJo. Maybe Chairman has both our bads.

'Good and bad everywhere,' she continues. 'But in rats. Urgh. All they are is bad. They like to eat everything.'

'Well, what is so bad about that? I like to eat everything.' Almost. I look at Peggy's belly sticking out from underneath her and am going to say she likes to eat everything too, but I don't.

'Yes,' Peggy lifts her head up. 'But rats run over all the pots and sacks and any food in the galley and make everyone poorly. They enjoy it as well.'

'Why?'

'I don't know. Maybe they think if there are no humans and no dogs and no anything else they'll be able to run around and do whatever they like. Do you know what poisonous means, Simon?'

'No, I don't.'

'Poisonous means making something go bad. Well, rats are poisonous. And they like it.'

'Oh.' I don't like the picture of that. I don't like the picture of wanting to make a thing go bad. That isn't very nice. Maybe Chairman is poisonous?

'So you really think I should stop rats?' I ask Peggy.

'Not stop them, Simon. Kill them. Make them die.'

I shudder again.

'I don't know if I can.' My whiskers droop down and I look at the floor.

'Fear not, my little friend. For I have a plan.'

My eyes brighten up at the sound of that one.

'Do you? Do you really?'

'Oh yes. Now I don't like those rats at all. I have seen them run all over the sailors' food and it makes them poorly. The rats leave a bad smell everywhere and, when they see me, they just laugh and run away.'

'So why don't you run after them?' I ask, my little pink nose twitching. 'Why don't you chase them?'

'Because... because... ' Peggy shuffles around. 'It doesn't matter. But they are beastly little vermin and, between you and me, I think we can ki— stop them once and for all.'

'How?' I look at her.

Peggy gives a little cough and shuffles around again. 'Well, I haven't quite worked that out yet to be truthful with you. As I have said, I am a doer and you are a thinker. But I am quite sure that, with a bit of thinking and a lot of doing, we will fight those evil rats and we shall win.'

And with that, Peggy closes her eyes and goes straight to sleep.

I lift my leg up and give myself a lick. It helps me to think sometimes when I do that. I think perhaps I have a lot of licking ahead of me.

Simon on board HMS Amethyst
Photo courtesy of the PDSA

6/ Pokerface

The sound of Peggy snoring in her box in this room - the stowage, that's it, I'm getting much more good at remembering things - makes me want to not be here. I climb over a bag, out of the room and find my way onto the deck. After I have been on the stern to do my conderate business - I know what Peggy means now, I have watched her and smelt it - I run under the huge chain and scamper up the stairs onto the quarterdeck.

There are lots of men up here, even more than in the mess deck. Some of them are whistling, some of them are rubbing the boat making it all clean and some of them are using brooms like the one the woman in the alley chased me and Uboat away with. There are soap suds everywhere with lots of different coloured lights wiggling in them. The soap suds go 'pop' when I bat them with my paw. I spy George and run over to him, my feet slipping out from under me as I run through the soapy suds.

George wipes his brow as I reach him, bends down and gives me a stroke. I rub against him. I want him to know I like him, but also that I like being in this place as well. On this ship. The Amethyst. What a funny name.

'My, my Simon, that was certainly one close shave, eh? Maybe I should lay off some of that demon drink in future. It doesn't half get me into a lot of trouble.'

I walk in between his legs and purr, happy that he seems happy.

'Good job you made a first rate impression on Lieutenant Griffiths.[18] Now, if you can just set to work on killing those darned rats we'll all be happy. Felt a bit sick myself this morning.'

'Hey, George,' a sailor with a big mark on his face calls over. 'How about we stick your little friend on the other end of one of these,' and he holds up one of the brooms. 'We'd get this deck clean in no time.'

My ears go right back.

'Ah, put a sock in it, Conway,' George shouts over to him.

'I'll sock you in half a jiffy,' Conway calls back.

Why are they talking about socks? George must notice my ears as he says, 'Ah, don't worry about him. They don't mean what they say. Most of 'em come from Wales, you see. Darned strange breed. Not like you.' And he strokes my back again.

'So, what are you going to do with yourself, eh?' he continues. 'Relax out here or start to work on those bloomin' rats?'

I give a little shudder again. I think I might wait for as long as possible before I start doing that. Or until me and Peggy come up with a plan anyway. I wonder what we could do.

I lick my paw and give myself a wash as I sit and carry on watching George and the other sailors for a while. I don't see Ginger or Gurns or McCunnell. Not that I want to see McCunnell, thank you very much. There is something about him I don't like. He doesn't make me feel as nice as George. And even though these men all look a bit different - some of them have short hair, some of them have a bit more hair, some of them have hair that is dark, others have light hair and some of them even wear round white hats - they all look the same to me as well. They look the same because they all seem to be smalls like me.

When I first looked at George he looked very sort of shiny and fresh and clean, even though his socks were very dirty and he was smelly, but when I see the other sailors, most of them look as if they have not been around for very long either. Like me. I wonder if they have more big brothers too. Or small brothers. Have any of them known people who have... gone? And when will they be gone too? I hope it is for more long than JoJo. I know JoJo had seen lots of things, like the Black Christmas he told me about and the time that did not sound very nice with the bang,

---

[18] Lieutenant Commander Ian Griffiths DSC and Bar joined the Merchant Navy aged 17, transferring to the Royal Navy in 1939. He served in World War II and joined the HMS Amethyst circa 1947. He was a cat lover and extremely fond of Simon.

bang, bangs when he had to hide, but I wish he had not stopped. We could have carried on playing and playing for a long, long time. I close my eyes.

I hear an angry shout, open my eyes and see McCunnell rushing towards me with a broom. I can feel all my fur stick up as I spring to my feet and dash off the quarterdeck. I scamper down the stairs and hear a yell behind me. As I turn round I see McCunnell slip right over and fall on his bottom. I hear howls of laughter from the men cleaning the quarterdeck as I reach the bottom of the stairs and turn to run up the - starboard - side. Yes, I'm getting much more good at these names now. Under a rope, in between here, over a... thing... and now I am at the front - the bow. There are some sailors up here too. One of them is looking at a huge bit of paper with all sorts of squiggly lines on it and another is scratching his head.

I don't quite know what to do next, so I just stand there and stare for a while then decide to explore the bridge, even though Peggy said I shouldn't. I trot through a doorway and take a look around. There's lots of paper, paper everywhere. Oh, I want to jump on it all. I really, really want to lie on it, it looks so... mmm. I am just about to jump on some of the paper when the door opens. It is the Captain. Oh dear.

He doesn't notice me at first. Instead he sits down and looks at all the paper. He is holding something in his hand and moving it around. Lots of marks appear on the paper as he moves his hand.

I give a little mew and he looks up.

'Ah, Seaman Simon. Managed to catch any of those pesky rats yet? Good. Good.'

I pad over to him.

'Just making some plans for when we finally make a move tomorrow. Oh gosh, I've just thought of something. You're not a spy are you? Sent here by those damned Communists?'[19]

What on earth is he talking about?

'I expect you want a drink?'

---

[19] The Chinese Civil War began in 1927 and ended in 1950, although the two warring factions united in 1937 to form a Second United Front to counter the Japanese invasion. The civil war was resumed in 1946. The war represented an ideological split between the Left Communist Party of China and the right Nationalists loyal to the Republic of China. The conflict eventually resulted in two de facto states, the Republic of China (ROC) in Taiwan and the People's Republic of China (PRC) in mainland China, both claiming to be the legitimate government of China.

The Captain gets up and goes through the door. I follow him and we step into a large room. It's very warm and nice in here, like a big hiding place. I can see a table and lots of things on shelves and comfy things for me to curl up on.

'Make yourself at home,' the Captain says and turns around as I jump onto his bed. 'Ah, I see you already have. Jolly good.'

There is a white and gold hat upside down on his bed so I get into it. He fetches a glass and a jug like the one before with the water in, only this one contains something dark. He looks over to me.

'Whiskey? No, of course not.'

He fetches me some water and pours it into a cup before pouring some of the dark water into a glass. He puts them both onto a table next to the bed. I notice there are some things in like the ones I fished out earlier. I can see them more well now. Maybe I should put my paw in?

The Captain sits next to me, reaches for his drink and knocks it back. I get up out of his hat, pad over to the table, put my nose into the cup and lap up the water.

'I say, have you ever seen these?' and he pulls something out of his starboard pocket. It is like a very smooth painted rock, with dots on every side. I get back into his hat next to him on the bed.

'This is called a die.'

I swallow. I don't like the sound of this.

'I use it sometimes when I'm caught between the devil and the deep blue sea.'

Hmmm. I know where the deep blue sea is, but where is the devil?

'Darned useful for making decisions sometimes, this is,' he continues. 'Sunk more than one U-boat with this, I have.'

Oh dear. This is getting more bad.

The Captain throws the hard thing across the room. It rolls and rolls before coming to a stop. Not a stop. It just doesn't roll anymore.

What does he want me to do now? Find Uboat, sink him and then die?

I look at him. He looks back at me. He stands up and pours himself another drink of dark water.

'Ah, that's a shame. My Monty used to run after a die all the time.'

I have heard that some me's do that. But that isn't really, um, me.

The Captain is muttering. 'Used to pretend I was playing poker dice with him.'

What is this? Some kind of game?

I decide if he throws it again I will jump down after it. I know if I was a dog I would probably just run over, pick it up and drop it at his feet without thinking. I have seen them do that before. But I am not a dog. I'm sure that's what Peggy would do if she was here. Actually, I bet she would just eat it. I think of JoJo and how he used to love running around after a ball. He would have done it.

The Captain picks up the thing again - the die - sits back down on the bed and rolls it between his fingers. I can smell his breath and I notice his eyes are quite red.

'One for sorrow. Two for joy. Three for a girl, four for a boy... I hope you're a boy, Simon,' he chuckles. 'Did George check for that? I knew you were as soon as I saw you, but O.S. George, bet it didn't even cross his mind.[20] Now, where were we? Ah yes. Five for a wish. I wish. I wish I was back home in darned England, that's what I wish. Six for a... I can't remember what six is for.'

It drops out of his fingers and, as it does so, I knock it with my paw onto the floor. The Captain looks down.

---

[20] Ordinary Seaman.

'Six!' He exclaims. 'Good lord. I'll make a player out of you yet. And with a pokerface like that I'm sure we'll make an absolute darned killing.'

Gulp. That word again.

'Here, let's try it again.'

He gives the die back to me and once again I knock it onto the floor with a paw.

'Oh, my goodness. I don't believe it. A six again. Talk about luck.'

I look at the dots on the die and back at the Captain. Now, I'm not really very good with numbers, but I'm sure something has just happened. Although I'm not sure what.

The Captain is sitting on his bed pouring himself another drink.

'This is darned incredible. I'll just... ' He knocks the dark drink back. 'I'll just... ' He falls backwards onto his bed. His eyes close. That snoring noise.

I look around. I quite like it in here. In fact I like it in here a lot. There is no smell like in the lower deck. Well, there is. A different smell. The smell of the Captain's breath is in the room, but it makes me feel quite sleepy. Maybe that's why he... yes, it makes me feel very sleepy indeed. I think I'll, I'll get back into his hat and... that's it, round and round and down and... aah...

JoJo is running around and around and up and down a green, green hill. I am on the hill too. The hill is moving, rolling from side to side, but I like it. Lots and lots of different coloured fish appear from over the hill and swim past me. I bat them with my paws, but they just spin, spin away. Now another fish appears with all fire and fog coming from out of its fishy mouth. It swims right up to me; it is getting more big and more big. Lots of fog and fire. I look around for JoJo, but he has gone. I am on my own again. The fish is right up close to me now. I am surrounded by fire and fog. It opens its mouth to eat me up and I...

I open my eyes with a jolt. It is quite dark in here, but it just means I can see that the Captain has gone. He will not be wearing his hat though because I am still in it. I wonder where he has gone. I wonder what Captains even *do* apart from walk around and tell people what to do and make fog and drink dark water and roll a die.

I get up, stretch and jump off the bed. I think I will go down to the shop and see if I can get any food. I go over to the door, but it is closed. I sit back down. At least the floor is nice and warm. I could curl back up again. Or I could look for the die and play with it. I look for it, but it isn't there. So the Captain has gone and the die has gone too. Maybe he has drunk some more of that dark water and he is trying to show Peggy how to play that game. What was it called again?

I hear footsteps outside so I cry out. Sometimes humans tell me to shut up when I make a noise so maybe they will now, and when they come in I can escape. I make a noise again. The footsteps stop and the door opens. It is a man I do not recognise.

'Evening, Simon,' the man says. 'The Captain said you would be in here. He told me to bring you this,' and he puts down a plate with some lovely food on. Then he puts his hand out to me. 'I'm Weston. First Lieutenant.[21] Pleased to make your acquaintance.' What does he want me to do with his hand? I stare at him until he walks out before I turn to the plate. I sniff it and then have a little nibble. Yum. I eat some and then leave some. I often do that, even when it tastes very nice. Like now.

---

[21] First Lieutenant Geoffrey L. Weston.

Weston has left the door open so I skip out and run back, back, down the stairs, along the ship and get to the stern. The stars are twinkling above my head. I run into the lower deck, wrinkle my nose and find George on his swinging bed. He is sitting up as best as he can in the little hiding place. Just like the Captain, he is holding something in his hand and making marks on paper.

'Where've you been, Simon?' he asks, rubbing my head. 'I heard you got into a spot of bother with old McCunnell today? He's a bit slippery that one,' and George laughs to himself. I jump up on his knee. 'Ah, careful,' he says. 'I'm just writing a letter back home. I miss home.' He points to a picture of some humans. They are all wearing more clothes than the other ladies. I look back at him and his eyes are all wet.

7/ Best laid plans

Me and Peggy have just been to see Pauloni. He gave us some nice titbits. Then he shooed us away because he said he had lots to do as today is a big, big day. I know what 'day' is, it means when it is not dark time, but I'm not sure how one day can be more big than another one.

The sailors are running around all over the place, busy, busy. They are all cleaning and moving things around or talking or scratching their heads like I do sometimes with my back leg. They don't rub my or Peggy's head though or even say hello. Not even George, but I notice his eyes aren't wet anymore. Maybe if he makes the deck all soapy and clean and then rubs his head it stops them from getting wet? Maybe it is just when he makes wiggly lines on paper that that happens, so perhaps he should just not put wiggly lines on paper?

Peggy says it is because we are going to sea soon and that is why everyone is busy, so it is best if we just hide. She said I will like it when the ship sets sail. I have seen ships and boats come in and out of the harbour, so I know what it is like to watch a ship when I am on the dock, but not what it is like when I am on a ship and not on the dock. I am going to go from where I am from to where I am not from, I suppose. I wonder if I will see blue birds and green birds like Uboat told me about. I can feel a flutter in my belly, but I don't really know what it is because I am not hungry. Not after having a yummy titbit off Pauloni anyway.

I tell Peggy.

'Maybe you have butterflies in your stomach?' she laughs as she clambers out of her box in the stowage.

I don't, I really don't. The last time I ate one of those, it really tickled and I could barely breathe. It was almost as bad as when I sometimes sicky up a ball of my own black fur.

'Or maybe it's the rats,' Peggy continues. 'I have seen them again running around all over the food in the kitchen. All over the rice and where they make the bread. So have you come up with a plan as to how to put a stop to all their beastly activity?'

'Well... ' I've been trying my best not to think about it. I was hoping a picture might come into my head when I closed my eyes as I went to sleep on George last night. 'We could always maybe try... talking to them and ask them to stop?'

Peggy throws her head back and wuffs. 'Ha, ha, woof, ha, Simon. That really is the most awfully preposterous idea I have heard for a long, long time.' She laughs and wuffs some more. 'Have you ever tried to reason with a rat?'

No, I haven't. Back where I am from they used to leave me alone and I used to leave them alone.

'No,' I tell Peggy. 'Me and my... we just used to play away from them.'

'Well, let me tell you, they really are the most dreadfully sneaky creatures. The Captain said we must kill them and that is what we shall do.'

I look at the floor and feel a flutter in my stomach. A slightly different one this time.

'Oh.'

'No 'oh-ing' about it. And there I was believing that you would come up with a master plan. Dear, oh dear,' and she shakes her head a little. Some spittle flies from her mouth onto my head so I have to lick and clean myself straight away.

A huge noise makes us both jump. It is as if all the men in the world have shouted at us at once. The stowage starts to shake too.

'That's the engine!' exclaims Peggy, wagging her tail. 'We must be setting off. Wuff, wuff, what fun!'

I run outside with Peggy following not so close behind. Both of us have to squeeze past the huge, huge chain because it is moving and rattling. It looks like a big, big snake and the sound of it hurts my ears. Now the whole ship seems to be shaking. It is very noisy indeed. Rattle, rattle, shake, shake. The whole ship is getting more hot too, especially under my paws.

'Quick, let's run up to the bow,' barks Peggy. We run up the starboard side, over... that... under here, through here and get to the stairs. Up we scamper right onto the bow. I look down and I see the big tongue has gone. There is nothing now between the ship and the port, my home. This is it. My heart jumps and thumps. I could not go home now even if I wanted to. Could I jump into the sea and swim back?

No. As I think, I realise that I do not even want to. This is the start of my new adventure. The start of me being brave.

I feel the whole ship start to move, except it feels as if someone or something is pulling me by my bottom. We are moving, but it feels as if we are moving bottomwards instead of forwards. How funny. Slow, slow we move. It is not as noisy up here on the bow as it is on the stern. I turn around and can see the Captain and a few other men on the bridge. The Captain sees me, gives a little shake of his fist and waves.

As we start to move I look down onto the dock and can see a group of humans waving at us. There are some smalls playing too. They are playing with a ball and they are throwing it and trying to get it into a box. I see a picture of me and JoJo and of how we used to play that game as well. The picture changes from a game into a plan and I feel a sudden burst of happy inside me. Now we are pulling away from the dock. The ship tilts a little. The noise changes. Another roar and then, yes, I can feel the ship moving forward and away from the dock.

I look out at the harbour and think of my plan some more. I look over at Peggy. She has her eyes closed and her tongue is hanging out. I look up and see some birds following the back of the boat. They are all squawking, but I can't tell what they are saying. I am flying away from where I am from even more fast than they are.

The sea, the birds, the Captain, Peggy. Bye bye where I am from. Bye bye horrible Chairman. Bye bye JoJo… I stare straight ahead and try to blink the water out of my eyes. It is just splashes from the sea. We are moving up and down too. It is as if the whole ship has turned into a big swinging bed. I am moving from side to side, up and down. It feels very strange. I look at the dock getting more small and more small. How funny, as we sail through the harbour, its walls on either side get more close and more big.

My heart is pounding, pounding. I wonder if this is what Peggy feels like and if the Captain feels like it as well. I can feel the breeze and I listen to the ship hum and rattle. It smells all fresh. I am going somewhere new, but I don't know where. A little bit of spray splashes up and hits me on the nose again. This is more exciting than scary. I only wish - I try not to think of him because the bad picture will come back again - … was here too. We could be having a new adventure together. This new adventure. This new life.

More spray now, some in my eyes and a little on my nose. I taste it. It tastes a little bit like the stopped fish. I would not want to drink much of it. It is a bit windy and I shiver, from the breeze or from being excited,

I don't know. Now we are sailing right in between the walls on either side of the harbour. Right through them until we reach the big, big sea. The clear blue water ahead, the bright sky above.

I don't think I have ever moved this fast before, not even when I have had to run away from scary things. My ears are right back, but that is because of the wind. This is fun, fun, fun! Peggy smiles at me. 'Like a picture waiting to be painted.' I don't really know what she means by that. She turns to look back, at the harbour behind us, at the port and at the hill leading up to the quarry.

'A scene of a landscape long since dried,' she remarks.

Me and Peggy stand there for a while. Then she turns to look at me.

'Are you enjoying yourself?' she asks.

'Oh, yes,' I reply. 'I could stand here for all of this big day.'

'So could I. But I'm afraid we both have some work to do. All play and no work means... well, I don't really know what it means, but come on.'

We run back to the stern, but it is still very noisy and now it is quite smelly too so we run up to the quarterdeck and hide.

'I think I've had a picture,' I say to Peggy.

She looks at me slightly puzzled. 'You mean you've been thinking? So have I. I've been thinking about food.'

'No. A plan.'

'Jolly good. What is it, dear Simon? Do tell... '

So, over the noise of the engine and under the bright sky, I tell her.

'By Jove, I think you've got it!' she exclaims. 'I knew if we put our heads together we could come up with something.'

Now it is my turn to look puzzled. I don't remember putting my head next to hers when I came up with my plan.

We head back to the stores again. I am on the counter, walking up and down and turning around as Pauloni strokes me. Peggy jumps up and puts her paws on the counter. Pauloni keeps giving us lots of titbits, but we are not eating them. Every time he turns around to fetch us some more we drop them onto the floor. He is talking to us both.

'Aren't you both lovely? Yes you are! You with your licky tongue and you with your gorgeous fur. It would make someone a most fabulous coat,' he laughs and gives me another stroke. 'I don't know what

I would do on here without such *bonaroo* friends to keep me company.[22] And what would you do without me? I bet you'd have *yeute munjare* that's for sure.'[23]

'What's *yeute munjare*?' I whisper to Peggy.

'He means 'no food',' she answers. 'He talks like that sometimes.'

I decide to purr as Pauloni carries on talking to me and Peggy.

'And I can tell you like being on here,' he says to me. 'Yes, you do. I remember my first time on board a ship. The USS Hope it was. Lucky 7, they used to call it.[24] It was lucky for me a few times, that's for sure... ' and he laughs, turns and gives us both another treat.

Peggy gives me a look and gets down from the counter. I notice she gathers up some biscuits and other treats in her mouth.

'Try not to eat any,' I whisper to her.

'I'll try not to,' she mumbles, her mouth full, and she trots off, but I can tell she is looking a little sad. Shortly afterwards she comes back. When she does so, I jump down from the counter as well. Between us we both carry all the yummy bits of food away. It takes a long time.

'Well done,' I smile at Peggy.

'Yes,' she answers. 'And I didn't even eat any either. Well, perhaps just a nibble... '

At dark time, after Peggy and I have had a snooze, we meet again in the stowage. It is nice and warm in here now. She clambers out of her box and looks at it. 'I hope this works,' she remarks.

We break up the biscuits into small pieces with our paws. Then, making sure all the men are snoring, we trot through the lower deck and

---

[22] Pauloni is speaking polari, a language used by the navy and homosexuals, amongst others. Omi-paloni means gay man and palone means woman. *Bonaroo* is Polari for wonderful.

[23] As Peggy explains, it means no more food.

[24] An American hospital ship, nicknamed Lucky 7, launched in 1943 and decommissioned in 1946.

through to the galley, carrying the small pieces in our mouths. We drop some of the broken titbits onto the galley floor, run back and fetch some more. We drop bits of food all the way from the galley, right through the lower deck and along to the stowage.

'Like Hansel and Gretel,' Peggy mutters.

'What's that?' I ask her.

'A fairy story I heard someone tell some little humans once,' she answers. 'Or maybe I saw it.'

I don't really know what she means. Never mind. In the stowage, Peggy drags her sleeping box over near the door. Between us we tip the box over so we can get in it from the side instead of having to climb into it. We drop more bits of food from the doorway all the way to the box. Peggy hides behind it while I hide near the doorway. It is like we are playing a game. Only a game where we have to wait for a long time.

The more we wait and the more hot we get makes me want to sleep. I don't know if there is less noise because the ship is moving or if my ears have just got used to it. I look over to see where Peggy is hiding. I can hear her snoring.

'Peggy, wake up,' I miaow loudly.

'Sorry,' she mumbles. 'I was miles away.'

No she wasn't. She is right here with me. Dogs are very odd.

We wait and we wait. I tell Peggy to make a noise every so often so I know she hasn't gone to sleep again. After my eyes have closed and opened, closed and opened, I hear a sound. Quiet at first before getting more loud, a snuffling and a squeaking and then a scrabbling of feet. I shrink back and try to hide some more.

Suddenly, I see not one, but two rats. Pink noses, like mine; pink feet, not like mine; and long thin tails, not like mine. They smell of not very niceness too. The first rat is very big. Very big indeed. His eyes are very small though. The rat behind him is more small. They both come in more near, nibbling at the broken biscuits, moving forwards, forwards until they are right next to the box.

Blam! I spring forward and jump in front of the doorway, blocking their way. At the same time, Peggy stands up and knocks the box over. It falls forward and traps both rats inside.

We've done it!

Peggy and the crew
Photo courtesy of Lieutenant Commander Stewart Hett

8/ Caught

I can hear the two rats running round and round inside the box.

'What do we do now?' I whisper to Peggy.

'Why, we wait of course,' she answers.

'What? For them to... ' I look at her.

'Yes,' she replies.

Gulp.

'And then we do it again and catch some more,' Peggy continues.

I can't help but feel a little bit sorry for them.

'Maybe we could just talk to them?' I suggest.

Peggy shakes her head. 'Tsk. Oh dear, oh dear.'

'How long will it take for them to stop moving?' I ask Peggy.

'I have absolutely no idea,' she answers. 'A few days, I suppose.'

I try and think how long that might be. It sounds like it could be for a long time. 'And do you really want to sleep in here when they are... doing that in the box?' I don't think I would like to do that. Not at all.

'Hmm. Mmm,' she answers. 'I think I would rather have my box back.'

I give a little tap on the box. The rats stop shuffling around.

I put on my best, scary voice. 'Hello, rats.'

Peggy looks at me. After a pause one of the rats replies in a thin, reedy voice.

'Yeess...?'

'What would you like to do? Would you like to stay in the box until you... or do you want to talk to us?'

The rats shuffle and mutter.

'We will talk to you. Yeesss,' the same rat squeaks.

I motion to Peggy and she bites at a corner of the box and manages to lift it up a little. As the two rats crawl out from under it she positions herself in front of the doorway so they can't escape.

'Who are you? Sss,' the big rat looks at me, its black eyes squinting.

'I am the king of all the rat catchers,' I reply. 'Who are you?'

'I am Mao Tse Tung,[25] leader of the Rats Liberation Army,' the big rat answers.[26]

'We could have left you in there, you know,' I say. 'I could catch all of you rats, if I wanted to.' I puff out my little chest to make myself even more big.

'Just try it,' the other rat sneers, but Mao Tse Tung flicks him with his tail.

'Would you like me to catch all of you?' I continue. 'I'm very good.'

Mao Tse Tung shakes his head.

'I have a plan. If we promise to give you some food, do you promise to stop running around all over the galley?'

'And why would we do that? Ssss.' Mao Tse Tung hisses again.

'Because we let you go instead of leaving you trapped. And because if you make all the men ill then there won't be any more food. And if there isn't any food there won't be any of *you*.' I'm quite enjoying all this pretending.

Mao Tse Tung lifts his head in the air and gives a little sniff. 'OK,' he answers. 'Rat's promise. Ssss.'

'Is that a deal?' Peggy asks him.

Mao Tse Tung looks at the floor. 'Deal,' he replies finally.

---

[25] One particularly huge rat that used to roam the Amethyst, nicknamed Mao Tse Tung by the sailors on board.

[26] A pastiche of the People's Liberation Army, part of the Chinese Communists who will become part of the story later.

I hear Peggy give a little sigh. But I do not want them to stop. I want to let them go. Chairman could have let JoJo go. But he didn't. I don't want to be like Chairman.

And with that, Peggy shuffles to one side and the rats scuttle off, their tails between their eight little legs.

'You sounded awfully funny,' Peggy says, licking my nose.

'Funny or scary? I wanted to sound like a king.' I give myself a little scratch.

'I'm not sure. I don't know what a king sounds like.' Peggy lies down. 'Do you think that will stop the rats from running all over the food and making the men ill?'

'I don't know,' I answer. 'Do you?'

'I've said it before. And I'll say it again. You cannot reason with a rat,' Peggy mutters.

'Maybe you can if you are king of the rat catchers,' I purr. 'We will just have to see. But it means me and you will have to do a lot of running around and getting bits of food. No more eating everything.'

'I suppose so,' she replies sadly.

'And at least you've got your box back,' I smile.

She puts her head inside. 'Although it is most awfully smelly.'

We lie on the stern and look out. The ship is rising up and down, but I like the way it makes me feel. The sky and the sea are all I see. I don't know if big-small is a word but that is how I feel. Peggy wuffs at me to show me the white waves trailing out from behind the ship as it cuts through the water. It looks like a long white tail.

'Would you still jump in after me if I fell in?' I ask Peggy.

'Oh, yes,' she replies.

'Even though the ship would be moving fast away from us?'

'Um. I hadn't really thought about that. Maybe if I barked very hard they would hear us and come back.'

Hmmm. I'm not so sure. It is still quite noisy. So noisy that I do not even hear the footsteps of McCunnell and another sailor creeping towards us.

'Thought you were supposed to be catching rats,' McCunnell jeers.

Suddenly, before I even have a chance to spring away, he lunges forward and grabs me. My little legs dangle down between his arms and he is holding me tight, tight. Then he dangles me right over the side of the ship. Peggy barks and barks, but he doesn't seem to notice. I can see the water just below me and feel the wind as the ship races through the water.

'Do you fancy a swim?' he laughs. 'I could throw you right overboard and nobody would ever know… '

I don't like this. Not at all. My heart is beating fast, fast. It is dark as I close my eyes and then bright as I open them again, staring as the sea rushes past me below my paws. Peggy runs over, growling, and I hear her bite into McCunnell's leg. He goes to kick her away, but she keeps hold of her grip.

The other man is just standing there. 'Eh,' he says eventually. 'Leave them be.'

McCunnell steps back and drops me onto the deck. Peggy lets go of his leg. 'Grrr,' he says at us and we both shoot off under the stairs, run round the place of the huge chain and to the other side of the ship. We are both panting and my eyes are full of water.

'My goodness, are you all right?' Peggy asks me. 'I really tried to bite as hard as I could, you know. He didn't even taste very nice either.'

'Thank you, Peggy. That wasn't very nice at all. I really thought he was going to throw me over.'

'Maybe we should go back to Mao Tse Tung and tell him to attack McCunnell in his sleep. He could make him as sick as a dog for all I care,' Peggy pants.

I wonder what she means by that. That she wants McCunnell to be ill like a dog she knows? Having a picture of a bad thing happening to someone bad, is that good or not? And didn't Peggy say there was good and bad everywhere and in all of us? So there must be some good in McCunnell somewhere. But there was none in Chairman.

My pictures are stuck between good and bad and the open sea. I blink, twitch my nose and decide to go to the bow. And also to keep away from McCunnell as much as possible from now on. As I stand there with the wind whistling through my ears, the Captain appears.

'Ah, the open sea,' he says to me and gives me a little stroke. 'I only wish my dear Monty could have joined me out here. You've already seen more things than he ever has.' Me and the Captain stand on the bow for a long time. Sometimes he puts things into his mouth and fog comes out of it, but I am not scared by it anymore. He also has a very big pair of long, round things that he puts up to his face and then looks around. After a while, he turns and goes back onto the bridge so I follow him. As I get to the doorway I stop.

'Oh, do come in,' he says. 'You *are* allowed. Captain's orders.'

I trot through the bridge. There are some men in there. One of them is standing beside all the papers. It is the same man who gave me some food and let me go when I was trapped in the Captain's cabin. He did that to me and I did that to the rats. How funny.

'Making good progress are we, Weston?' the Captain asks.

'Aye, sir. We'll be reaching the Malaya Straits right on time.'

'Good. Good. Any reports of any activity?'

'Three ships sighted off Penang sir, but they're contained,' another man replies.

'Well, I'll send a message out to them to offer our assistance if needed,' the Captain continues. 'Meanwhile, if anyone needs me, I'll be in my cabin.'

'Very good, sir.'

The Captain enters his cabin, removes his cap and places it on the end of his bed. I jump up onto it as he pours himself a drink of the dark water. I listen for the familiar clink, but I don't hear anything. Then he lies on the bed next to me. It is very comfy on here and in this cabin. Much more so than in the lower deck with all the other smelly men. And where not very nice McCunnell is of course. I think I may just stay here for the rest of this big day. And it has been a big day too. But for now I think I will just move around a little and... aah. That's it. Perhaps later on I could go into the galley and hide somewhere and see if the rats creep in and run around on all the food? Yes, I might do that but, just for now, I will...

The Captain rubs my head. 'Dog's life, isn't it?' he smiles at me.

Oh dear. I'm all confused again.

9/ Pops with stars

If I sleep in the Captain's cabin in his round white and gold hat - in *my* hat - the pictures I have when I close my eyes are mostly nice. When I sleep on George though, in the stuffy lower deck that gets more smelly every day, the pictures are mostly bad. But even though I like to sleep in the Captain's cabin more, I still sleep with George as well, because he found me and brought me on here, and that is more good than the bad that is in the pictures. And if ever his eyes are wet he likes to stroke me and that makes me feel nice as well. So, even though I think he must be seeing bad because of his wet eyes, I know there is good when he strokes me.

I am lying under a table in the mess deck with Peggy. George is sitting at the table with Ginger.

'Haven't seen King Rat in the galley for a while,' Ginger says to George. 'Your Simon must have polished him off.'

I don't know about polished. But every night time - I know now it is called that when it is not day - me and Peggy leave some food that is yummy and food that is sometimes not so yummy out near the stern. And when it gets light and the men are all out of their swinging beds and working, the food has all gone. We can smell that Mao Tse Tung has been too. Peggy says he is our enemy, but I just think that he is not a friend. Friends and not friends. From and not from. Peggy and George - friends. McCunnell - not friend.

Not that I spend much time on the stern. Peggy likes to watch the white tails, coming out bottomwards, I suppose. I like to be right on the bow, looking out. Can it really be all big, big sea everywhere, all the time?

I even like the noise the ship makes. Sometimes I picture lots and lots of me's, as many as I can all purring at the same time, but I'm still not very good with numbers so I end up picturing one big me instead. My fur is stiff and sticky all of the time too, no matter how often I lick my paw and try to clean myself. Sometimes, when George is having a wash, I sit there and watch as he gets all wet. I like it more now when the splashes land on me, but I still would not like to run through it.

I am getting more good at fishing the things I can't see out of a jug of water. I do it whenever some of the men like Ginger and Gurns do not look happy. It makes them laugh. It still makes my paws cold though. Pauloni in the stores is always very friendly. He is from a place called America. That's where Uboat has been. I wonder which way America even is from here. And I wonder if Uboat has been here in the place where the sea is everywhere.

Where we are now is the South China Sea. I know that because George told me. I like to look out here in the daytime where I can see lots of nothing. Even at night time when the sea and the sky change colour and the stars come out, I lie out on the deck and wash myself and let pictures come in and out of my head.

As I lie under the table near George's feet - they are not so smelly when he has his big black boots on - the jimmy comes in.[27] I know his real name is Weston and that he is the First Lieutenant because he told me that when he brought food for me to the Captain's cabin, but the sailors all call him 'the jimmy', even Jimmy sometimes. Funny how even humans can have more than one name too. When George told me about Weston being called the jimmy I thought of how JoJo used to call me Titch, but on here they call me Simon. And sometimes Blackie. Jimmy is always on the bridge helping the Captain and they talk together a lot.

'Captain says there's action in Malaya,' Jimmy tells George and the others sitting there.

'Why, what's happened?' someone asks.

'Gent has declared a State of Emergency.[28] Three factory owners in Perak. Killed.'

---

[27] Navy slang for first lieutenant.

[28] Sir Edward Gent was the Malayan Governor and Colonial Administrator. He declared a State of Emergency when three British plantation owners were killed on 16th June, 1948 leading to the Malayan uprising. The Malayan Emergency, as it was subsequently called, was so named rather than it being referred to as a war, because Lloyds of London were the underwriters of many of the British owned and controlled factories and plantations. Their insurance wouldn't pay out in the event of war.

I swallow.

'Who killed them?' George looks at Jimmy.

'Reports say it's Lau Yew.'[29]

One of the older men spits. 'I remember that name. Leader of the MPAJA. Bunch of bandits they were.'

'What's the MPAJA?' George asks the older man.

'The Malayan People's Anti Japanese Army. Darned rag bag bunch.'

'Only now they're known as The Malayan People's Anti British Army,' Jimmy chips in. 'Want us all out they do.'

'So are we still on patrol duties or heading to Malaya?' the older man asks.

'Still on patrol duties, Atkins. Any suspicious looking boats, we stop 'em. Don't want 'em supplying the insurgents,' Jimmy explains.

Anti Japanese. Darned rag bag bunch. Insurgents. What strange long words humans use sometimes. I hope I don't have to remember any of these.

'Ah, would have liked to see some action,' Atkins clenches his fist.

'Strictly monitoring, this mission, Atkins. And supporting the Malayan regiment if they need us.' Jimmy turns to walk away. 'Simon,' he looks at me and smiles. 'The Captain wants to see you.'

I run alongside Jimmy until we get to the bridge. He bends down and rubs my head before I pad into the Captain's cabin. He is sitting in a chair, rolling the die between his fingers, a drink in his other hand.

'Ah, my good man. Do come in. Everyone treating you well I hope? Good.'

How I wish I could tell him about McCunnell.

'Thought you might want to play a little game,' the Captain says cheerfully.

---

[29] A member of the Malayan Communist Party, leader of the Malayan People's Anti Japanese Party, guerillas who were opposed to Japan's invasion in World War II and later, that of the British, hence the name change to Malayan People's Anti British Army. The Malayan Uprising / Emergency has been attributed, in part, to Lau Yew.

I jump up onto his knee, almost spilling his drink. Of course I would like to play a game. I always do. I can't imagine a time when I wouldn't want to run around and play.

'I'm going to throw this again,' he waves the die in front of my face. 'I'm going to roll it three times and if we get a six you can have a lovely treat.'

Oh good. I know what treats are, although the nice man in the stores calls them bennies.[30] He uses lots of other funny words too.

'Do you think I can do it?' The Captain laughs. 'Of course I can.'

He leans forward a little and throws the die onto the floor. It rolls and comes to a stop.

'Oh, damnation!' He sits back and slams his knee with his hand. I shuffle further up then, as he stands to collect the die, I drop down to the floor and run over to it. I give it a little sniff and a knock with my paw. As I do so, it rolls to one side.

'I don't believe it!' he exclaims. 'You've done it again. No need to roll it again now. Just wait there a moment,' and he walks fast out of his cabin.

I sit there, not quite sure what to do. I hope I'm not in trouble. I lick my paw and wash my face as I wait.

The Captain enters again with a big smile, a tin can and a bowl. 'You'll like this,' he beams. 'I got one of the men to get some for you just before we set sail. Have you heard of Lane Crawford?'[31]

I stare at him.

'A most excellent outlet it is. The owner imports goodies from all over the world. English tea, chocolate biscuits. I only feel sorry for those back home still on rations.'

He places the bowl on the floor next to me, sits down and produces something from his pocket. He uses whatever it is to dig into the top of the can. He moves the can round slow in his hand and continues to do whatever it is he is doing. At one point he even makes a little squealing

---

[30] Navy slang for a treat or reward, derived from 'benefit'.

[31] A high end boutique store founded in Hong Kong in 1850 which was selling luxury imported British and other goods such as tea bags. Today it is a retailing company with specialty stores selling designer label luxury goods in Hong Kong, China and online.

noise and puts his hand in his mouth to lick away some of the red that has appeared. I start to think of JoJo again and the sticky stuff that was all over him but, as the Captain takes the top off the tin, the pictures of JoJo are replaced by a most yummy smell.

'Here,' he says, scooping out some of the contents from the tin into the bowl next to me. 'I'm sure you're going to love this. Whiskas,' he says.[32]

I'm not sure why he says that. I already have whiskers and I know they are not brown and they don't smell like this. I stand up and stare at the bowl with the brown food in it. I circle around it slow, sniffing and letting the smell go up my nose and swim around my head. It smells so yummy it almost makes me feel dizzy. I do not know what it is. What could it be? Whatever it is, it is most definitely good and not bad. If it was bad then I would just wrinkle my nose and walk away of course. But oh no, it isn't that, it isn't that at all. It is good, good, good! A part of me wants to just put my head right in and eat it all up, but another part of me wants to just sniff and wait and, mmm, sniifff...

Maybe when I put my head in and try it, it will not taste as good as it smells, so then I will just feel sad. But maybe I could put my head in and take a little nibble and it would taste even more good than the promise of it as it tickles my nose? This most lovely smell coming from the brown food in the bowl in front of me is making my head spin now. One more slow dance around the bowl, a little dip of my head and... Shall I? Shall I do it now?

I put my head right into the bowl, do a big breathe in, feel my tummy go big, stick my tongue out, take a little lick and... Ooh that is the most best thing I have ever tasted in my life, much more good than the stopped fish back home. My head pops with stars like in the sky at night time and my tongue seems to melt and disappear. I take a mouthful, swallow and feel the most best good food in the world slip down my throat, into my belly and send a shiver all the way right down to the end of my tail. Another little bite and - oh yes - I feel it right down to the end of each of my paws.

I want to run round and round in circles, jump high, high into the air, get right into the bowl and cover myself with this lovely, yummy brown food. I take another sniff before I have some more. Mmm, just as good. I could eat and eat this until I get as big as Peggy. More big. I

---

[32] Perhaps the Captain is psychic as 'Whiskas' cat food was called 'Kal Kan' in his day, but 'Whiskas' fits perfectly here so artistic licence has been taken.

wonder if she has ever tried this. Or even knows what it is. Maybe I will tell her. Maybe I won't and just keep it all to myself. And one thing is for sure, Mao Tse Tung is definitely not going to have any.

I look up at the Captain and he is smiling, smiling. Why isn't he eating any of this? I'm sure this brown food is even more nice than the brown drink he likes. Another taste and chew and swallow. And another. Shall I eat it all up quick or more slow? I don't know. All I know is this is where I want to be right now, more than anything else. On this ship. With George and with Peggy and the Captain. And this lovely, lovely, yummy brown food in the bowl.

'See,' the Captain says. 'I knew you'd enjoy it.'

10/ Shadows and monsters

Me and Peggy are scampering from the stowage to the stern. We did our condeederate business when it first got bright, and our job when it began to get more hot. We have been collecting little bits of food from here and there, from Pauloni or from the men who drop us little titbits in the mess deck. Bully beef and rice, bread and biscuits, it all goes to the stern for Mao Tse Tung and his friends so they don't make *my* friends ill.

Now we are playing, even as it gets more hot and even more hot. We run round and round the ship. All along the starboard side, right up to the bow, down the stairs, along the port side to the stern and round again. I want to chase Peggy, but it is easy to catch up with her, so I get her to chase me instead. She can never catch me though, so sometimes I run more slow just so she can. Her tongue is always hanging out as she pants and pants and her tail is wagging, so I know she is happy. My tail does not wag when I am happy. I wonder why hers does and mine does not.

I can jump around and over things easily too. I love to spring up and crawl under whatever is in my way. As we run and play, I look starboard and out across the sea. Far, far away, just where it ends, I can make out a dark shape. It looks like a small black cloud has come to rest right on top of the sea.

'Look,' I call out to Peggy. 'I can see something.'

She comes running up to me. 'So can I. I can see the sea.' She gives a little snort.

'No, no. Over there. Look.' I try to get Peggy to see where I am staring.

She looks and sniffs and looks. Then she shakes her head. 'I think you must be mistaken, dear Simon. There really is nothing out there.'

As she says that, Ginger and Gurns appear. Gurns puts his hand above his eyes and squints.

'Land ahoy,' he beams.

'Malaya,' Ginger cries. 'We must be in the Straits now.'

So that's it. It is a place I can see. Land. Called Malaya. I wonder what it's like.

'Are we going to go there?' I ask Peggy.

'I shouldn't think so,' she replies. 'Jimmy said we're just on patrols.'

That's a shame. It might be interesting to see another place. A place where I am not from. I wonder what the humans would be like in that place. And the birds. And the food of course. I stand there and look out at the dark shape. At Malaya. What happens there? Is it more good than bad?

I find a small patch of shade out on deck and lie in it to keep out of the hot sun. Peggy flops onto the deck, her tongue hanging out. She is still in the sun though. I watch her get more hot and more hot. Her paws look like George's wet eyes, as if all her feet are crying. Little drops of water run down and form a small pool on the deck. Her tongue is hanging out as if she wants to drink the air. The sea is the same blue as the sky, hard to even tell where one stops and the other starts.

'We're in another painting,' Peggy pants, looking at the blue all around us.

'What's a painting?' I ask her.

'Like a picture,' she replies.

She must mean like the pictures I see in my head. Sometimes, when I close my eyes, the pictures I see are the same as when my eyes are open. Other times, the pictures are replaced by different things. Of where I am from and times when I was happy. And occasionally, when all the men are snoring, the pictures are of not very nice things. Of scary eyes and of big things and things that are hidden. I tell Peggy.

'Sounds like spooky shadows and monsters to me,' she remarks. Then, 'Oww.' She must realise how hot she is under the sun because she stands up slow before squeezing next to me to get into the shade.

'What are shadows and monsters?' I ask. 'They don't sound very nice.'

'They're not,' she replies. 'Shadows are like this,' and she looks round at where her body is. 'In the shade, here. That's a shadow. Caused by the steps.'

'Oh. And what's so not very nice about them?'

'Well, sometimes they are good. Like now. But sometimes... erm, have you ever thought you could see something and then when you look again it has gone?'

'I don't know,' I answer. 'Maybe. Sometimes.'

'Well, that's a shadow. It can be there and then it can be gone. Like monsters.'

'But what's a monster?' I look at her. I like these little stories, but they are a bit scary as well.

'Monsters are big scary creatures that come and jump out at you. They hide and they lurk and just when you least expect it... waah!'

My skin trembles inside my fur a little. 'How do you know about all of these things?' I want to know.

'Because my master told me,' she answers, yawning.

'Oh. And who is your master? Is it Lieutenant Griffiths?'

'Heavens, no. I didn't always reside on this ship, don't you know.'

'So where *did* you live?' I ask, my ears pricking forward.

'I used to live in a most wonderful big house. There were lots of rooms and comfy beds. And I had lots of toys. My favourite was a blue sock monkey.'

Ah. Monkeys. Uboat said he'd seen them. 'What's a monkey?' I ask Peggy.

'Monkeys are very soft and cuddly creatures,' Peggy replies. 'My toy monkey was, anyway, so I suppose they are in real life as well. I don't know. I'd love to meet one though. I used to chew and chew my monkey until he only had one ear left. 'Ere 'ere,' she chuckles. 'We had a most magnificent garden too.' I look at her. 'And, before you ask, a garden, dear Simon—' She lifts her head up and looks out over the sea. 'Well, it's a bit like that, only a different colour. Big. *My* garden was anyway.'

I'm still not really sure what she means. Maybe Peggy means like water to play in. But how can you run around in water?

'And was it just you and your master who lived in the big house?'

'Oh, no. He had a wife and some... I know you call them smalls, and we also had a lovely maid who used to do everything. She would wash and cook and clean. She used to give me lots of nice food all of the time. I would go for long, long walks with my master. He used to throw me sticks and I would chase after them, bring them back to him and he would throw them again.' Peggy's back legs twitch as she tells me this.

'Throw. Run. Catch. Run back. Throw, run, catch, run back...,' she continues.

75

I close my eyes and I get the picture, I really do. I have seen dogs do that before. I always wonder why they do that when *I* don't want to. It seems a bit silly to me. I know I might do it for the Captain sometimes, but that is just because he seems to like it. Maybe that's why dogs always do it with their masters, to make them happy?

Peggy shakes her head quickly, as if trying to stop herself from falling asleep.

'Anyway,' she continues. 'Something happened to my master and we stopped going out for long walks. The maid still used to feed me but, instead of going out, I just used to run around in the garden. Then I stopped running around so much. I don't know why. Instead of the master throwing me sticks, he used one to walk with instead. I used to fetch it and chew it and drop it at his feet, but it was no use.'

'So what did you do then?'

'We used to get into his car and we would drive to something called a cinema,' she answers.

'What's a simena?' my head starting to ache a little with yet another difficult word.

'A cinema is like a big, big room with a huge moving picture in that you watch. You can see and hear, but not smell or touch. It's as if you are there, but not there.'

There and not there? Now I am really confused.

Peggy must notice because she tries to explain some more.

You watch pictures and you can feel it inside of you but not outside. It's like a waking dream, if the pictures you see are good. If not, they are like waking nightmares.'

'What sorts of things can you see?'

'Anything really. Big men and women and cars and places. Things you see every day. But also the sorts of things you might only see when you are asleep. Awfully frightening things. Frightfully awful things.' Peggy gives a little snort.

'You mean… '

'Yes. Monsters and people jumping out from hiding places and doing bad things to each other.'

'And do they ever get you?'

'Oh, no. They are just in the big moving picture. I used to close my eyes sometimes, but jump if there was a huge noise. My master used to laugh or cry, but sometimes he would jump or fall asleep too.'

'Then what happened?'

'I woke up one day and he wasn't there anymore.' Now she looks sad.

'At the cinema?'

'No. Back in the big house. It was just his wife and the, um, smalls. But one day they weren't there anymore either. It was just me. People came and chased me so I had to run away. Well, not run. Move quite fast. All I had was my monkey.'

I don't really like this story now. It is making me feel sad too.

'And then what?'

'Well, I don't really know. Somebody found me and gave me to the Captain. He brought me and my monkey on board this ship and I have stayed on here ever since.'

Is that what humans do, I wonder. Do they find us and look after us? Well, that must mean they are good. Mostly good. I think of McCunnell.

'Where is your monkey now?'

'I don't know.' She looks sad again. 'I think the Captain might have lost it or it might have fallen overboard or something.' She stops herself from looking sad and tries to jump on me, but I spring out of her way.

'I'm a monsterrrr!' she laughs.

'Ha ha. You're not a monster. I know what you are. You're a dog.'

'Grrr... ' she growls and tries to scare me, but it doesn't work because it is warm and bright and I know who and what she is.

'So are monsters real?' I ask her, still not quite sure.

'Well, dear heart, that depends what you mean by real,' and she rolls over, gives a little parp and falls asleep.

I am still confused. Real is what I can see and hear and feel and touch and taste and smell. But at the moment I can't see George, yet I know he is still real. And I know I won't see JoJo again. So does that mean he isn't real? Of course when I close my eyes and go to sleep and see pictures I see him, so maybe he is just real when I am asleep. And sometimes I see mother too, even though I don't remember smelling her or cuddling up next to her. So does that mean she is not real?

And what about pretend? JoJo used to say the planes back home with the bang, bangs used to be pretend, but they were also real too. Oh dear, too much thinking makes me want to go to sleep too. I get up and scamper into the lower deck. I know the sailors are on deck so they won't be asleep, so I give a little jump when I hear, 'Hey, Simon.'

It is Gurns, lying on his swinging bed. 'You've caught me having a quick you-nap.' He reaches down and strokes the top of my head. 'Are you going to sleep too?' I lie on the floor next to him. 'To sleep, perchance to dream. I love dreaming I do.'

He tells me a lot of the time he dreams of his sweetheart back home. I purr as I listen to him. A sweetheart is someone who you like the best. He says he loves her and wants to be with her forever. Love. I wonder what that is. But if it is to do with somebody that you want to be with all the time then it must mean it is a good thing. Love must mean that humans see pictures like me, like when I see JoJo. And love must be something you want to be in forever. So it is nice to be able to close your eyes and be with who you love.

As Gurns is telling me about his sweetheart and love and I start to see pictures, I can feel my whiskers droop and my eyes start to close. I do not mean to, I did not think I wanted to, but it is so hot and I have been so busy today running and playing and purring. I stretch and yawn and... ahhh...

To sleep, purrchance to dream.

11/ Singapore strife

Behind is the big blue sea, stretching out maybe forever. Above there are some birds that have joined us, flying and screeching above the ship, as if they are saying hello. Ahead I can see land and buildings getting more close and more close.

Lau Yew, the bad human that Jimmy spoke of, has been stopped.[33] Really stopped. They all cheered when Jimmy told them about Lau Yew. I just licked my paw ready to give myself a nice wash, not really sure what all the fuss was about. Then they cheered some more when the Captain said some of the men could have some leave when we finally dock here.

And here is called Singapore.

As Singapore gets more big, I think it looks a little bit like Stonecutters Island. There are lots of boats and ships in the harbour. Some of the humans on them wave as we pass. As we sail into the port and finally stop moving, I spy some boats with little eyes painted on their bow.[34] I don't know what they are called and I only wish my brother was with me now to tell me their names. I'm sure he would know. I wish he was here anyway, having these adventures with me out at sea, feeling the

---

[33] Lau Yew was killed by British security forces on 16th July, 1948.

[34] 'Bumboats' or 'lighters' were, and still are, used in the Malay Archipelago to carry supplies, cargo and, more recently, people.

79

wind and the spray. Or hearing birds say hello when we come to a new place.

I look up at all the white buildings that line the harbour, stretching off into the distance. Some of the men on the ship are lined up too, standing straight and excited to be getting off. Then I give myself a good old wash; I lick and clean every leg and my face. I want to be all ready for this new place, even if it might be a bit scary. I look up and see George with Peggy by his side.

'I'm a bit scared about this,' I say to Peggy as she comes up to me. 'A new place. We'll be all right though, won't we?'

'Oh, I'm not coming,' Peggy replies. 'I'm getting a bit too old for all that walking around malarkey. Oh no, I think I'll just stay here. I might just relax on the deck and, you know, eat and sleep.'

My whiskers droop a little. That's a shame. I want my feeling of being brave to be more big than my feeling of fear. And that would only happen if I get off the ship and go and explore with Peggy.

'Hey ho, Simon,' George says and lifts me up. 'Some of the lads are going to buy some gizzits and have a bit of a drink up.[35] Do you want to come too? Wiggle out of my arms if you don't.'

I just lie there in his arms. If I'm with George then I'll be safe.

'Good,' he continues. 'You can come with me to post these first,' and he waves some things he is holding in front of my face. I go to sniff them, but then the Captain shouts and I jump.

'Attention!' The men all stamp their feet together - how silly, I wonder how they planned that trick without talking to each other - and fall quiet.

'Crew,' the Captain barks. 'The time is now fifteen hundred hours. Enough time to collect some supplies and have some R'n'r.[36] All personnel to report back on board at twenty-one hundred. No exceptions. And no women!'

'What about a quick trip to Bugis Street, sir?' Atkins asks and the men all laugh.[37]

---

[35] Presents.

[36] Military abbreviation for rest and recuperation.

[37] The red light area of Singapore at the time, well known amongst sailors.

'There'll be no catching the boat up on my watch,' the Captain answers and someone slaps Atkins on his back.[38]

'Dismissed,' the Captain shouts and the men all break out of their lines and troop down the long tongue, talking and laughing. I feel as if I am surrounded by good and happy. Once we step onto the dock, George sets me down on the ground. My legs are all wibbly wobbly as if I am still on the ship.

'I think we'll go this way,' he says and heads off away from the dock. I run through many humans' legs to keep up with him, trying to look at all the stalls selling goodies as I do. They are selling yellow, curved things; green round things. Everything smells fresh. When we turn into a street though it all changes. There are lots of pretty trees that make it less hot, but there is some water running next to the street. It is very dirty and very smelly indeed.

'Ah, those must be storm drains,' George says, picking me up again. 'I've heard of those.' We stop and stand next to a girl who is watching a man standing in the water. He is very thin and brown with cloth round his head. What a strange place to put it. He is rubbing, rubbing his mouth and teeth with something and using the water to rinse.

'Urgh, look at him cleaning his teeth in that filthy water,' George remarks.

Cleaning teeth? I know I like to keep myself clean, but I never think of cleaning my teeth. How would I do that? I know I certainly wouldn't use dirty water like the man is. As we stand there watching, a huge, huge snake, much more big than back home, appears from nowhere and slithers right between the man's legs. He drops whatever it is he is using and runs away, screaming.

George laughs. 'I bet he wasn't expecting that.' Neither was I. I am glad that George is carrying me. I know that snake would eat me up in one go if it saw me.

The girl taps George on the shoulder. She has brown skin like the snake man and big brown eyes.

'Excuse please. I looking for my friend. Have you seen her? Her name Maria Hertogh,' and she holds up a picture of a human, just like the ones George has next to his swinging bed.[39] He looks at it.

---

[38] Contracting a sexually transmitted disease.

'No, we haven't.' He gives a little smile. 'But we are not from here. English.' George's face goes bright red when he speaks to the girl, as if he has just been in the sun.

She nods, stands back and looks George up and down. 'Ah, sailor,' she laughs, then she looks at me. '*Kuching*.'[40] As she goes to stroke me under my chin, George coughs, his face still red.

'Do you know where we can post these?' he asks her.

The girl looks at them, looks puzzled for a minute, but then breaks into a huge white smile.

'Ah, yes. Come. Come,' she answers.

George laughs and his face becomes less red again.

We follow her and head down an alley.

'Do you live here?' George says to the girl, pointing around him.

'Yes,' she answers. She looks like I do sometimes when I don't want to play. I forget the word.

'What is name?' she asks George.

'George,' says George. Looking just as... shy, ah yes, that's it. 'And this is Simon.' He gives my head a little rub and I purr.

The girl smiles. 'My name Ah Soo. You like Singapore?'

'Not sure yet,' George answers her. 'I think so.'

'Singapore is nice,' she replies. 'People here, very friendly.'

We come to a little shop.

'Here,' Ah Soo tells us. 'Please. No.' Then she points at me and shakes her head before stepping inside.

'Oh, righty ho,' George sets me down on the ground outside the shop. 'It looks like you're not allowed in. No blacks, no pets and all that.'

What does he mean? I'm not black. I'm black and white. And am I a pet? What is a pet anyway?

George and Ah Soo step inside the shop. I sit outside and wait, hoping that a snake doesn't come along. I look up and see lots of clothes

---

[39] A Catholic girl raised by Muslims, who was eventually returned to her biological parents which led to extensive rioting in 1950.

[40] Malay for Cat.

on bamboo poles hanging out of windows. They stretch all across the alley, high up. They look like flags. It looks like back home. I shrink back as close to the shop as possible as many humans' legs rush past, as bicycles weave in and out between them and nearly run into me.

As I look back up at the clothes, I can see some... I don't know what they are... swinging about. One of them pulls some washing down as it climbs down the walls, swinging and jumping. They look like tiny furry smalls, not quite human. I can hear noise, not quite talking, more like lots of birds all screeching at once. They are getting more close to me now. I wish George would come out. My fur stands on end and my nose quivers. I want to run into the shop, but Ah Soo said I could not go in. Now my whiskers and tail are standing straight out too.

They are coming more close now; they have dropped onto the ground. One of them has seen me and shows me its teeth. This is not good. They come over and circle me. They move more slow and I can hear them sniff and see their noses move. I do not like this at all. Maybe these are the monsters that Peggy told me about? I start to shake, my heart thumps and I can smell them, smell them coming towards me.

One of them makes to grab me. I jump out of its way and try to scamper through them, but another of them catches me by my fur. I yelp and then yelp again as its nails dig into my back. It shakes me and hugs me close to its chest. Suddenly, they all set off running through the alley, the monster pressing me tight against it. Some humans point and laugh at us, but I know this isn't funny.

The monsters and me turn sharply into a wide street. Bicycles and cars rush past us. I can feel the hurt of the monster's hands now pressing down on me, its nails digging right into my back. My heart is pounding, pounding and there is a rushing sound in my ears. I let out a squeal. Where is George? I want George. Or JoJo. I should never have left Stonecutters Island. I should not have left the ship. I should have stayed on there where it was safe. What use is it being brave?

I can feel myself going upwards as we clamber up one of the trees; up, up. The trees are not so pretty now. Human heads and the top of cars are below us. I have not been this high before and I do not like it. This is not like flying. The monsters are all around me. I am thrown to another one. He catches me and strokes me hard. Too hard. These are not friends.

Maybe I could bite them? But what if they bite me back? I give my best hiss, feel my fur stand on end and my tail stick straight out, but one of the monsters just grabs it. What are they going to do to me? Are they going to eat me? Where is George?

Some of the monsters are pulling the green off the trees and eating it. Some of them are grabbing sticks and dropping them down below. None of them are letting me go. I am trapped. Trapped like the rats back on the ship, but I haven't done anything bad. I cannot tell what these monsters are saying. They just make scary noises. I don't like it here. I don't like Singapore.

Suddenly the biggest monster runs down the tree and the rest all follow. I am being pulled down, down. We get to the bottom and run back to the road. Where are we going? What are they going to do to me? Maybe they know the snake and they are going to give me to the snake? Or maybe they are going to do to me what Chairman did to JoJo? I have never been more frightened. Ever.

As we run across the road I hear a shout over the noise of the cars. I see the big wheel of a car going round and round, moving fast before - bang! I feel it. We are no longer running. Me and the monster tumble over and over in the road. I realise the car has hit the monster and it has let go of me. Quick, quick. I jump onto my feet, spy the other side of the road and run and run, dodging in between the wheels of the cars and the bicycles. I look over, but the monsters are not coming after me.

But I keep running and running, more fast than I have ever run. I run round a corner, under a fence, jump over a... I don't know what... before turning another corner and finding a wall. Phew. I am shaking and my whole body is pounding. I am very sore on my back. I crawl behind the wall and hide there, panting, thinking, panting. I am lost. I am thirsty. I am scared. I don't know what to do or where to go.

I lie there and wait. Hidden away from the road and away from the monsters. If I stay here then this is a new place where I will be. A place that I do not like. If I move, maybe, I don't know. But I know that I want to be on the ship more than I want to be here. Perhaps if I walk slow and follow my nose I might be able to find George again? Or the smell of the storm drain might help me?

Very slow, I stand up and sniff. I cannot smell anything I recognise, but I know I have to walk and keep walking. I head down the street, looking up and around all the time to see if the monsters are still around. The sun is hot on my back, making it even more sore.

I walk and walk until I get to a big white building. Lots of shiny black cars are driving to the building and slowing down. People are getting out of the cars. Some of them are wearing hats. Men get out of the front of the cars and walk round to the back. They take bags out and walk up to the grand building, up the steps and inside.

I scamper over to the big patch of grass in front of the building. There are lots of smalls playing on it. I come to a tree, look up to see if there are any monsters in it, find a nice patch of shade and settle down underneath it. My back hurts, but it feels good to be out of the hot sun, to smell the grass and be away from everything and everyone. Almost everyone.

I watch the smalls to see what they are doing. Some of them are running with things in their hands. They look like small flags and, every so often, the flags go up in the air and stay there for a short while before dropping to the ground again.

I think of JoJo again. What would he do? I think of the place where I am from. Do I wish I was back there? I don't know. I don't know if I would like to be there if JoJo was not. I think I would like to just be on the ship. With Peggy and the Captain, with George and the others. On the ship I have my job and my friends. I have my games that I play with the Captain and with the other men, the die and the cold things I cannot see. Here, I do not have anything. It is full of scary monsters and snakes. I start to cry.

Then I start to yowl. I have not made this noise before. Some of the smalls even stop playing and look over. This is a different sort of cry. One I have not made before. I feel, I don't know, I feel that if I saw the monsters again I would just scratch and scratch them. What is this feeling? I close my eyes and wish I was not here. I try to pretend the grass underneath my feet is the road in the port back home or the cold, hard floor on the ship that me and Peggy make the 'clack, clack' sound on. But it does not work. I know where I am. I am here, all alone, with no one to snuggle up to or play with.

I open my eyes very slow. The smalls are still playing, all happy, happy. But I am not happy at all. I do not know where to go or what to do. If I lie here and think then maybe I will have a picture and I will know what to do. I think and think, but a picture does not come. Maybe I could go into the building? But why? I look over at the building and then at the black cars with humans getting out. As I do I think I see a wobbly shape I recognise sniffing around the humans and looking up at the hotel. Wait a minute, I know that shape! Of course I do. It's Peggy! Dear old, wobbly, lovely, always hungry Peggy! Now I see she is with Ginger and Atkins. I jump up and run, run, fast, fast, fast across the garden and almost leap onto her back.

'JoJo! JoJo! You're here!' I am so wrapped up in happy, for a moment I even forget who she is.

'Why, yes.' She licks my face. I squeeze under her belly and come out the other side. 'When the chaps told me about this Raffles Hotel

I thought I must come and take a look.[41] It's awfully grand isn't it? Exactly the kind of place I would like to live in. And this beautiful garden. Heavens! It's just like mine back home.'

I don't see how this garden looks like the sea, but it doesn't matter because I am so excited to see her. Then Peggy stands back and takes a good look at me.

'My gosh, you look awful.'

Ginger strokes me. 'Thought you were with George? Oh crumbs, look at your back.'

But I do not care about my back. I don't even care if this place is grand or not. I just know that I feel safe and I don't want another adventure again. Not for a long while, thank you very much. I tell Peggy everything that has happened as we lie on the grass. She doesn't know what the monsters were and at first she does not believe me. She does when I show her the marks on my back though.

'Battle scars,' she remarks. I don't know what she means. She must mean my back.

When it becomes more dark we go to a place called Change Alley.[42] I make sure that Ginger picks me up and I stay in his arms all the time. The next best thing to George. He tells me and Peggy about everything we see as we walk past and as we settle down on some wooden stools.

I watch a man who is making some food for Ginger and Atkins. Ginger tells me what the man is doing. He points out the charcoal, a burner, a grill and some skewers. The cooking man stabs the meat with the skewers and puts them on the grill part. They spit and sizzle as if they are not happy to be cooked. The yummy smell soon gets into my nose and goes all the way down to my tail. It is called satay and, when it is cold enough for me to eat, I try it. It is the most yummy food I have had, apart from the food the Captain gave me of course. Maybe the monsters thought I was made out of satay?

---

[41] A luxurious colonial style hotel in Singapore built in 1887.

[42] In the 1940s it was one of the many busy streets in Singapore, full of cafes, stalls and hawkers selling their wares. It is now part of the financial district.

When we have finished eating and are leaving Change Alley it is getting dark. The lights of the cars light up like eyes and there are lamps everywhere, on the stalls and in the shops. I can still smell the storm drains a little bit, but I can smell the food being cooked all around even more. And I look to see if there are any monsters around. No, there are not. Phew!

We stop to watch some men who have cloth round their heads, just like the man me and George saw before. One of the men has a huge snake around his neck. Maybe it is the same snake as before? It hisses. I don't like it and cling to Ginger even more. But another of the men is moving cups around, which I do like. He hides something under one cup, moves them around and when he lifts the cup up, the thing hidden underneath has gone. The brown men with cloth around their heads are called gulli gulli men and Ginger says they are magic.[43]

'What's magic?' I whisper to Peggy.

'Magic is something which can't be explained,' she beams. 'Sometimes it is wonderful and sometimes it can be scary.'

Yes, I think. The ship. Here. All of it is magic...

---

[43] Egyptian entertainers.

12/ Full moon fever

The Captain is ill. I did not know what it meant when I heard someone say it. I suppose it means when you are sad or cannot move around very much. Then Peggy told me it means the same as poorly so I suppose I was kind of right. I have been scared before, hungry and thirsty too, but I don't think I have ever been ill or poorly. It sounds as if it is what JoJo was before he was stopped. The poor Captain spends a lot of time in his cabin, lying on his bed. Sometimes he calls me Monty instead of Simon. He does not want to play the rolling game with me or stroke me. His head is always hot and he drinks lots of the clear water and none of the brown water.

I still like to sleep in his hat though. *My* hat. At night time, whenever all of the men snore or when it is too hot or when it is too smelly, I get up off George, pad out onto the deck and creep into the Captain's cabin. I listen to him coughing and watch the little drops of water running down his face. Sometimes I lick them, but not all the time because they taste salty; the same as when the sea water splashes up and gets me.

I sometimes feel funny too, but I don't think it is because I am ill. I feel more happy than sad and I still want to run around. Sometimes I feel like I did when I was hiding in the garden of the Raffles Hotel, after I ran away from the monsters. I feel like I want to, I don't know, run even more fast, jump more high, purr more loud. I speak to Peggy about it, but she doesn't really know what I mean. Sometimes I almost feel as if we are as close as a brother and a girl-brother and then other times I think she doesn't understand me at all.

'We are like chalk and cheese, dear Simon,' she gives a little chuckle when I tell her sometimes I feel funny. That just makes me even more confused.

We have just finished dropping titbits up on the stern. 'Aren't you getting frightfully bored with this, dear heart?' Peggy asks, as I sit down and wash myself. 'I never thought I would end my days as a slave to some rotten rat.'

A slave? End of days? But it isn't the end of the day. It still has to get more hot and then more cold and then night time.

'What do you mean?'

'The Captain asked you to kill the rats, the filthy vermin, and instead here I am running around after them like... like an old maid.'

She looks a bit cross.

'Can't you, you know...? Don't you have it in you?'

I don't know what she means, but I know I must be doing something to make Peggy unhappy. Or not be doing something. She hasn't spoken to me like this before.

'I'm sorry,' she says finally and goes to give me a lick. 'I'm feeling rather unusual at the moment. Perhaps I'm getting ill like the Captain. I think I'll go back to my box and have a nice little snooze.'

Oh dear. I don't want Peggy to be all sad and not move around either. Maybe I should do something. Or at least try. Which is more good? Giving food to the rats so they leave the sailors alone or making the rats go away? I swallow. Maybe I should try, really try...

That night, after I have played with JoJo and we have run away from the scary monsters and a big snake with no eyes chasing us, I open mine, yawn, jump down from George and get away from the smell. I go up onto the bow, breathe in and look out. I can see stars and can just about make out a cloud. It seems to glow a little, as if there is light behind it. Except for a light coming from the bridge, up here the rest of the ship is completely dark. Good, I like it when it is dark. I can see, see as well as a, well, as a me. I breathe out. Can I do this? I really want to be brave.

I pad down the port side, over... that, under... this, down the stairs into the doorway and through... here. I am standing outside the galley. I lift my head a little and give a little sniff. My whiskers are all stood on end. Another sniff. What was that? Oh, nothing, I just caught a whiff of some of the food me and the sailors had eaten before. Quite nice it was too. I hide behind a bag of flour. Maybe I will see a rat, maybe I won't.

I stretch my front legs out and my claws. Am I ready for this? I wait. I smell something before I see it. A smell almost like the storm drains back in Singapore, but not nearly as bad. Not very nice though either. It smells of... it smells like. Yes! I smell a rat. A pink nose, long whiskers and pink feet run across a shelf just above my head. So they do still come in here! Greedy rats.

The rat jumps down from the shelf and onto the floor. It scampers across, stops and gives a little sniff. Maybe it can smell me too? It comes over right near me and the bag of flour. I coil, back hunched ready to pounce. My back legs are trembling a little, but I am ready, ready to spring and to jump and to catch the rat. To dig my claws into its back just like the monster did with me. I stretch my front paws again, give my nose and whiskers a little twitch and, and…

I can't do it. My legs don't seem to want to work. I cannot jump. The rat scurries away, squeaking as it runs through the doorway, out and away. I look down and stare at my paws. Is this what Peggy means? That there is something in me that I do not have? Yes, there is something, it is a something that does not want to make things stop. When I get my funny, new feeling I sometimes want to jump high up into the air or at monsters chasing me, but I don't want to be Chairman. I want to be me.

I creep back outside, up the stairs and onto the deck. One star is winking, blinking at me more than the others. I look at it and look at it.

'Be careful what you wish for,' a familiar voice behind me says. It is George, rubbing his eyes. 'I woke up and wondered where you were. Thought you might be in with the Captain.'

No. I have been somewhere else. Not doing my job properly. I give a little mewl.

'Ah, you sound sad. Come here.' And he lifts me up and gives me a cuddle.

We sit down on the deck. I look up at him and then past him. The cloud is not there anymore but the big, round thing I have seen before, yet do not know the name of, is.

'Can you see it, Simon?' George whispers. Why is he whispering? There is no one else here. 'I love the moon, I do.'

Ah, so that's what it's called. The moon. What a lovely name for a lovely thing. I know I don't see it all the time. Sometimes I forget to look up, but sometimes it is not there. Other times it is high up and small, or low down and big. Sometimes it is as if a part of it has been eaten. I wonder why that is. If George can see it though and knows it has a name, then at least that must mean it is real, even if it is not there all the time. Maybe it is magic. The wonderful kind.

'You know, when I was very small,' George says, 'Somebody said to me the moon was made of cheese and I believed it almost until the day I joined the navy.' He gives a little laugh.

Cheese. That was what Peggy said she was, or maybe I was. Does that mean the moon is full of me's? Or dogs?

'How do we know it's not made of cheese anyway?' George continues. 'Nobody has ever been there. I suspect they never will either.'

I give him a look.

'You know, sometimes I think you can understand every word I say.' He rubs me between my ears. 'I'll let you into a secret. When I get lonely and miss home, I come up out here on deck and I look at the moon. I wonder if everyone I know back home can see it the same as me. Are they looking at it and thinking about me?'

He blinks, strokes me again and I purr. We both look up at the moon for some time. I wonder if George has pictures in his head of everyone he knows back home looking up at it too. Then I think about how many dogs or me's might be living up there.

George stands up and makes for the stairs. I give a little wiggle and stretch my back legs out.

'Don't you want to go back in, Simon?' He looks at me.

No, I don't. I want to think about the moon and cheese. I want to think about if I am good or bad because I did not jump on the rat.

'OK.' He sets me down and disappears down the stairs.

I pad up and down a little. So what am I? I know I should make the rats stop. I should, I should. Peggy said a rat cannot be reasoned with and she must be right. Mao Tse Tung said they would not go into the galley and help themselves and he was wrong. I don't know what to do. If we keep on giving them food then Peggy will be unhappy, but if we stop giving them food they might just go into the galley more and more. If they do that then the men might all get poorly. Maybe that's why the Captain is ill? I hope not.

I hear a noise coming from the bridge. It is a horrible, moaning, groaning sound. I think it may be the monsters again, but I know none of them came onto the ship. I checked. What shall I do? I decide to scamper up, up the stairs, go up to the bridge and see.

I run up and in. Lying on the floor is the Captain. He does not see me, but he makes a horrible noise again. I circle round and round, sniffing him. He does not smell very nice. I tug his arm a little, but he just moves it away. I run back out, down the stairs, along the ship and into the lower deck. I jump right up onto George, put my face up to his and lick his nose. He stirs a little so I lick it and lick it again. Then I claw him and mewl.

His eyes open.

'What's wrong, Simon. What's the matter?'

92

I jump off him, turn and look back at him.

He swings his legs off the bed and follows me outside. I run, run, up, up to the bridge. When we get there he must not see the Captain at first because he says, 'What, what is it?'

Then George sees him.

'Oh, my gosh,' he exclaims and kneels down next to the Captain. His arms and legs are moving around and he is dripping, dripping.

'Sir, sir. Are you all right?' George puts one hand behind the Captain's head and opens the Captain's eyes with the other. The Captain makes a horrible, growling sound.

'Sir, can you hear me?' George gives the Captain a little smack across his face. I'm sure that's not a very nice thing to do. The Captain opens his eyes and stops growling.

'Uh, huh. Feel sick,' he says. 'Water.'

George rushes off and I run over and rub against the Captain's hand. 'Ah, there you are. Good boy. Fine boy. Aah. Urgh,' and he strokes me a bit too hard. I can feel his hand all hot and wet.

George comes back with a jug of water. Does he want me to play with the things I can't see?

'That's right, Simon. You let the Captain stroke you. Make sure he doesn't fall asleep. I'm just going to cool him down.' He feels around, finds what looks like a little white flag in his pocket, dips it into the jug and dabs the Captain's face with it. George disappears again before coming back with a glass.

'Found this in his cabin.' He gives it a little shake and pours some water in from the jug.

'Here, sir. Drink this.' George tips the Captain's head forward. The Captain manages to take a sip of the drink George is holding up to his lips.

'I think it's just a fever you've got, sir. When we get back into Hong Kong, we'll get a doctor to check you out.'

Hong Kong! That's where I'm from. Are we going back there? I wonder if it will still look the same. Or feel the same or smell the same. I know it won't *be* the same because of one thing of course. Will I even want to get off the ship when we get there?

George is still dabbing the Captain's face and making him drink. He looks a bit more awake now and a bit less scary.

'Where am I?' he asks.

'You're on the bridge, sir. You must have wandered out of your cabin.' George tells him.

'Good heavens. Surely not, no. Darn this damned illness. Do you think you and Monty here can get me back into my cabin?'

'Aye, sir,' and George manages to lift him up and half drag him back into his cabin and place him back onto his bed. The Captain goes back to sleep even more quick than Peggy.

'Good job we heard him, eh, Simon?' George turns to me. 'He might have tried to set sail when we were still anchored down.'

That must mean trying to move after being stopped. I know how not possible that is.

'Come on,' George says. 'I think he'll be all right now. I think you should stay with me for what's left of this night.'

We leave the Captain and his being ill, step out of his cabin, walk out on deck, under the moon and back into the lower deck.

It still smells. Of cheese but maybe not chalk. Not that I know what that is. I will have to ask Peggy what she meant by that when she wakes up. But for now, I will just try and cover my nose with my paw.

13/ Begging bowl

Forwards, forwards into Hong Kong harbour. Before, it was my bottom waving goodbye, now it is my head saying hello. A head that is much more full of things, more big words and lots more pictures than when I left. Scary things like monsters and McCunnell and snakes, more big than the ones that live on Stonecutters Island. Wonderful things like Peggy and George and the moon. I follow George around on the ship, and the moon follows me around too. It has chased me all the way back here.

The rats are still on the ship, the rats I know I must… get rid of. I told Peggy about going to the galley and what happened, but she just shook her head. 'I don't want to say I told you so, Simon, but yes, well, I told you so.'

So, I need to come up with a more good plan or be more brave than I have ever been before. The Captain is still poorly too. He has red blotches all over his body and lots of the other men are ill as well. The rats must be doing something to them. I am not poorly though. I just feel - what does Peggy say? - 'unusual' sometimes, although her unusual is different to mine. She just wants to sleep a lot. I want to pounce and scratch and jump.

As we sail back into the place where I am from, I can see the hill on my starboard side, not as green as when I left. The moon's brother, the sun, must have cooked it since I have been away. I hope it might have cooked other things that live on the hill too. I shiver after I have had that picture. I know it is very bad, but it is not nearly as mean as a very bad thing. A real thing that has happened yet still does not go away. I claw the deck and close my eyes.

When I open them I can see, yes, I can see where I used to play on my jetty. My nose twitches at the thought of going back there. The place where I used to wait for the humans to come back in their boats and throw me some fish. Will they say hello to me if I go back? More close, more close. Now I recognize where I saw the smalls throwing a ball into a box. The picture that became a plan that worked. I give myself a lick, pleased that I had seen JoJo and seen the smalls and they had helped me to do my job. Then I stop licking when I think of the rat in the galley.

I look up, but there are no birds. They must have all gone away to play. Funny I didn't see them when I was in the middle of big, blue nothing. I wonder where they go to. Maybe they go to Malaya? I don't think they will go to Singapore, not with the monsters there. Another shiver. My back is not sore anymore, but I don't have to close my eyes too tight to think about how sore it was.

I don't know why we have come back to Hong Kong or how long we are staying here for. I do know I would like to get off and have a sniff around again. I am not scared of doing that in a place I know. A place where I am from. Was from. Well, maybe a little bit scared. So long as I don't go up to the hill then I think I will be OK. Or maybe if I just stayed close to George or Peggy then nothing or nobody could get me. Yes, that's what I'll do. Here comes George now.

'You look lost,' he smiles.

Of course I'm not lost. I know exactly where I am.

'Jimmy says we just need to get the men sorted out and then we'll be off back to Malaya. Bet you know the way there yourself now, eh?'

It's out through there, into the blue, and turn port, not starboard.

'Bet you can't wait to get back on your old stomping ground either?' he chuckles.

As long as you come with me. How I wish I could tell him.

The ship has docked now and some sailors are moving the big tongue. Straight away, some men come marching up. They do not look like sailors. Jimmy puts his hand up to his head as soon as they step on board.

'Ah, he's here,' George remarks and walks over to them.

Some of the men are dressed in dark clothes and they are wearing hats. Another one is dressed all in white. He looks very smart. More smart than the Captain even. Another man is tall, carrying a bag and nodding his head a lot as Jimmy speaks with him. I wonder if I should go over and say hello. I start to walk over, but then stand still instead, watching.

Peggy appears, her tail between her legs and her tongue hanging out.

'My, my, this beastly weather. It's hot, isn't it, Simon?' She looks over at the men who have come onto the ship.

'Ah. Doctor, doctor. I've swallowed a roll of film,' she mutters.

What is she talking about? I scratch.

'Come back tomorrow,' she looks at me. 'And we'll see what develops.'

She rolls on the floor laughing, her tail wagging hard. 'Dearie me,' she snorts. 'I'm here all week.'

I look at her. 'Peggy,' I whisper. 'Are you all right?'

She stops rolling and sits up. There is spittle all round her mouth. 'Don't worry, dear, I haven't gone mad. Just a little joke.' She coughs. 'Ahem.'

What's mad? Or a joke for that matter?

'That's a doctor who's come on board,' Peggy explains. 'To check on the sailors and see why they're all so badly ill.'

'Isn't it the rats?' I ask, my head cocked to one side.

Her whole face seems to drop. 'I don't know. I've seen them get sick before, but not like this. I haven't seen those beastly red blotches before. Whatever it is, I hope it isn't catching.'

No. I don't really like catching things. But I thought Peggy might.

'Do you want to come and see where I am from?' I say. Peggy has moved away from me to settle in some shade away from the bright light and the hot sun beating down on the deck.

'Oh, no. It's far too hot for me.'

'Please, Peggy,' I mewl. 'I want you to see.' I don't really want to tell her I am just a little bit scared as well.

'Weeell. I could come I suppose. Will there be any food?'

I nod. I'm not sure where though.

'And drink?' Her tongue hangs out even more.

'Yes, I'm sure we will find something to drink as well.'

'All right then.' She stands up, her belly wobbling. 'Lead the way.'

I shoot across the deck and scamper down the tongue, get to the bottom and wait for Peggy. She trots down, slipping a little as she does so. 'Whoops. Butterfeet.'

'Come on. This way, this way,' I say to her. It feels good to have my paws back on a place I know.

I run, run down the dock, the water on my starboard, then slow down as I realise Peggy has not caught up with me. She is sniffing everything as she walks along. Come on, hurry *up*, I think. Many human legs rush past as I wait for Peggy. I had forgotten how busy it was here. I was wrong. It is just as busy as in Singapore.

I look out across the water. At the sampans and the junks tied up. There seem to be a lot more big ships sailing into the harbour too. Much more than when I was here last, when I left or, rather, when I flew away with George. It feels funny to be back. I suppose at the time I was too scared to even think about such things, shaking and frightened under George's arm. Now here I am showing my best friend the place I am from. One of my best friends.

Peggy finally catches up with me, her tongue hanging out. 'I need a drink. Where do you recommend?'

We wander down an alley. It is more cool here, but still busy. There are many humans going into shops, but they don't notice us, all getting on with their own lives, shopping and talking, laughing and smiling. We sit outside a shop for a while, but it is no use, no one wants to stop and feed us.

'Aw. Hmm.' Peggy's ears droop. 'We really must do something about this, Simon. Here, let's go this way.'

What? What is this? Now she is showing *me* around. We turn down another alley, one that I know of course, but I have not been down since I was a very small me. I know we are not near the less green hill though so no chance of bumping into you-know-who.

We get to a big shop. I can see lots of jars and tins piled up inside. Green, red and yellow things are in boxes outside. They smell very fresh and clean, but they are still not anything I would like to try to eat. There is a colourful thing, like a flag but not a flag, hanging over the shop so all the things outside are in the shade. To keep them cool, I suppose. Peggy stands back and looks up at the front of the shop.

'Ah, this is the place,' she turns to me and smiles. 'Follow me, dear Simon and do exactly as I do.'

Peggy trots into the shop and sits across the doorway. I sit next to her, right near her bottom. Then decide to move to one side, just in case. We look up and see the owner standing behind the counter, talking to another human. The owner glances over at us both, but she does not say, 'Shoo.' Instead she smiles at Peggy and Peggy makes her tail wag, before letting her tongue fall out and giving a little whimper. I stare at her and notice she has made her eyes go very big too. More big than I have ever seen her do.

I give a little mewl and try to make my eyes do the same as hers, but I can't do it.

'Make another noise,' Peggy whispers to me, so I let out another mewl, although it is drowned out by her more loud whimper. She scratches her paws on the floor too.

The human steps over us both, clutching a brown paper bag. Peggy makes sure to move out of her way.

'Good dog,' the human says, before walking away.

Peggy looks at me. 'Go on.'

I mewl again, like I did when I was trying to get JoJo to play with me.

The owner calls to us. 'OK, OK, I see you. And you brought friend with you too.' Peggy moves her tail and hits the floor with it. Thump, thump, thump. The owner comes over to us and bends down.

'Where you been?' She rubs Peggy's head. 'When you go to live here? You want drink?' Peggy wags her tail even more and I stand and rub myself against the owner's legs. Round and round I go, my tail sticking straight up. The owner laughs and rubs my head as well. Another mewl and another whimper from Peggy.

The owner disappears and comes back with two bowls, a red one and another one; I'm not sure what colour it is. She puts one in front of me and the other in front of Peggy. We both stick our heads in the bowls at the same time; lap, lap, lap. Peggy looks at me mid lap and smiles.

We soon drink it all. It was just water, but I forget how lovely it is when you are very thirsty. Peggy then stands up, moves away from the bowl and, with difficulty, rolls over on her back. Her pink belly flops to one side as she tries to stick her legs up into the air. It doesn't really look very nice, but it must do what Peggy wants it to do because the owner has returned with two more bowls, this time with meaty food in. Again she puts one in front of me and gives the other to Peggy. I smell a familiar smell, put my head right up close to the bowl she has given me and have a taste.

Oh my gosh, it's the same as the food the Captain gave me. Whiskers. I still think it is a silly name, but it is still the most yummy food ever. I wonder if the owner has given Peggy the same as me. I try to push her big head out of the way of the bowl so I can have a little sniff. It does not smell the same. She is so busy eating that she actually gives me a little growl. She must have forgotten it is me.

I chew and eat and swallow. Chew, eat, swallow. Peggy has already eaten hers and puts her head into my bowl to try to eat some of mine. I bat her with my paw. Eh! Get away! I eat more quick. I even feel a bit sick, but I do not care. There. All gone. Then I lick all around the bowl and finally rest my back legs by having a nice sit down. Sometimes I like to leave some food but, when it is a new place and I don't know if I'll be coming back, then I like to eat it all in one go.

Peggy is smiling at me again. 'Yum. Yum. Right, what's for pudding?'

The owner picks up our two empty bowls. 'You both very hungry. You not get fed where you live? Dear, dear.'

She rubs both our heads and I try to give her my best smile. Peggy licks her hand.

We trot out of the shop.

'That place is called—' I start to say to Peggy.

'Yes. Lane Crawford. I know,' she answers.

'But how did you...?' Is she magic?

'Us dogs know these things. Besides, I've been there before. Lots of times. Right, time for a nice little lie down, I think,' and she yawns. And then burps.

We turn back down an alley, into another one and keep walking until we reach a part of the port I know.

'Let me show you where I used to live and play.' I bite Peggy's leg. 'This way.'

'Oh no. I'm far too tired for that now. I think I may just head back to the ship and have a lovely snooze,' she answers.

'Come on, Peggy. Please.'

'Really, Simon, no. I have seen more than enough of this place thank you very much and, even though I'm sure it is lovely, it isn't anywhere near as lovely as having a nice sleep in the stowage when the engine has left it perfectly warm rather than too hot,' she pants.

'OK then.' I look a little bit sad. 'Do you know the way?'

'Yes, it's up this way.' She sets off, but I grab her by her back leg again.

'No. It's that way. Do you want me to walk back with you?'

'Of course not, Simon. What do you take me for?' And she trots off again, even more slow than when we first got off the ship. I watch her bottom and her tail disappear amongst all the humans before turning port and walking along the edge of the harbour and the sea. At least I won't have to wait around to see if anyone throws me any fish. I am far too full.

I skip over some ropes and round a cart. A bit of me hopes that someone will call out, 'Hey, Simon,' but then I remember that, when I lived here, I was not called Simon. Then I think of Chairman. What if he is prowling around? Or the grey me who overheard me and Uboat and ran off back to tell Chairman? Perhaps it would be best if I just follow Peggy and go back onto the ship where I am nice and safe?

Shall I be brave or not brave? I don't know what to do. I look at the ships that are sailing in and the boats that are tied up. Maybe I should do what the Captain does with the die? But I don't have a die. I can see a small boat sailing in now, but I cannot tell if the human in it is a man or a woman. If it is a man I will go back to the ship, but if it is a woman I will be brave and go to the jetty where I used to play.

I look at the sun glinting on the water, find a shadow so it is less hot and keep on staring at the boat. It bobs up and down, sails between another two boats. The human is throwing something over the side. As it gets more close, I can nearly make out what the human is now. A bit more close and, yes, it looks like I am going back to the ship because it is a... Oh no! It is a woman.

I swallow hard and stand up. Out of the shadow and into the light, before I turn port and pad behind a crate. I cross the road and hide behind the wheel of a car. I am looking around all the time, but there are no me's, only me. I keep walking and looking until finally I reach my jetty. I even find the place where George picked me up. It looks the same. I reach my favourite place where I used to hide in the sun. It feels strange to be back here. A place I thought I would never leave and then thought I would never see again. I feel happy that I have been brave to come here, but also sad that... someone is not here and will never be here again. Funny to be feeling all sorts of different things at the same time.

What's the word? Opposite. Oh yes, I remember Peggy telling me when I asked her about the chalk and the cheese. That is how I feel. I feel opposite. And full. And a little bit of that scratchy feeling as well.

Would I be brave enough to stay here forever and not go back to the ship? Maybe I could just stay here and pretend that George and Peggy and everyone else weren't real? No, I could not do that. Would not want to do that. Not at all. This may be the place where I am from, but I know that being on the ship is where I want to be.

I yawn, then I have a little stretch and I smile. It is quite windy. All I can smell is the salty air. It is nice to be here, but it will be more nice to get back on the ship too.

I hear a gruff voice behind me.

'What are *you* doing here?'

14/ The best a cat can get

My whiskers stick straight out. My nose twitches, sniffing the air for a scent. I move my head round slow, my body hunched. Am I ready to spring out of the way, or to leap forward and scratch if I need to? I turn, shaking, waiting to see the large, bad, grey me with one staring green eye… who is not there.

Instead, I am greeted by a jumping-around-trying-to-leap-onto-his-shadow-oh-my-gosh-it's-so-good-to-see-him… Uboat.

'Hello, Uboat!' I leap on him. 'You wouldn't believe where I have been. I have been on a ship and met a dog and been chased by monsters in Singapore. I went there but not Malaya. I have to chase after rats… '

'All right, slow down,' he laughs.

Then I look past him. There, standing at the top of the steps, I spy a lovely white fur coat. As it runs down the steps towards me and Uboat, I smell a scent that gets right up my nose and makes my eyes and head spin. It is Lilette, looking even more big and more lovely than before. Lilette, the only other nice me I know in the place where I am from - *was* from - is here, is here now. My head is still spinning.

I wait for my head and the pictures to clear and breathe out.

'Hi, Lilette,' I say to her as she gives both of us a quick sniff. 'Hello,' she replies. 'I'm not sure I ever knew your name… '

'It's Simon,' I reply. I still feel a bit shy around her, especially when I tell her my name. Even Uboat gives me a funny look when I tell her. I am sure I sound a bit more high than normal. This is the first time I have ever said hello to her and she has said hello back. I hope I don't sound as silly as I think I do.

'You'll have to use this ear though because I'm deaf in the other. And please don't say purrdon because I've heard it all before.' She flashes her teeth, but I know she isn't flashing them like those scary monsters did. They are very nice. 'I haven't seen you for a long time. Where have you been?'

I tell Uboat and Lilette all about Chairman and JoJo and George, making sure I stand on the starboard side of her so she can hear everything I say.

'Poor JoJo,' mewls Uboat and Lilette looks sad too.

I tell them about the Amethyst and Peggy and the rats. About McCunnell and the Captain. I make myself sound more brave when I get to the scary parts, but I'm sure Uboat can tell I am pretending just a little bit.

'So that's where you've been,' Uboat says, giving me a lick. 'I told you that ships were fun.'

'Most of the time.' I give him a nudge with my paw.

'I've been here for quite a few naps and some sleeps waiting for you. Lilette here said she had not seen you.'

Lilette stops cleaning herself for a moment and looks up. 'But I know where you've been now,' she smiles. 'You've been having lots of adventures.'

'And what have you been doing?' I ask her. 'Where is Chairman?'

Lilette tells me about the places where she plays. About a nice man and woman who give her food, so she goes there every day. 'I haven't seen Chairman though. I think he may have gone,' she says after a while. I wonder if she means really gone, or just not here anymore.

Then it is Uboat's turn to tell me about where he has been. About a big storm and having to sail somewhere so that his ship could be mended. 'But I'm sure you'll agree,' he says at the end. 'It is much more exciting having adventures than just listening to them.'

He is right. I used to love listening to his stories, but it is a lot more fun now I can understand more of the things he talks about and I have tales of my own. I have tales and a tail. How funny.

We all sit there for a long time, enjoying the feel of the hot sun, being together and knowing that Chairman is nowhere to be seen or found.

'I wonder where Chairman is then,' I say to Lilette again.

'Don't know and don't care,' she answers. 'But it is nice to play on the hill and know I won't be chased away.'

104

'I'd chase him if I saw him again.' Uboat bats me with his paw, but I know he doesn't mean any of it.

'Do you want to go and get some food?' Lilette asks us both.

'No, thank you,' Uboat replies. 'My ship will be going soon and I just know there will be some lovely food on there waiting for me.'

As we watch the sky get more dark, more ships are coming into the harbour.

'There's going to be a flotilla regatta,' Lilette says proudly, as if it has something to do with her.[44]

'What's that?' I ask. Uboat hasn't heard of one either.

We wait for her to tell us. Pretty Lilette who also must be very clever as she knows things that even Uboat doesn't know about.

'Don't know,' she says and me and Uboat both laugh. Me a little more than Uboat.

The sound of a ship's horn echoes all around the harbour. 'That's for me,' Uboat laughs. 'Well, it's not really for me, but I know I have to go.' He stands up. 'Lilette, it was lovely to bump into you and it was so wonderful to see *you* again.' He rubs my nose. 'I knew I would though. We always do.'

Uboat springs away. I watch him as he scampers up the steps, down, round and away. Yes, we always see each other again.

Lilette gets up and moves a little more close next to me. I start to feel strange again. As if I could jump right into the water and swim over to the ships. I can feel my heart pounding underneath my fur. Even my mouth has gone dry so I lick my lips. Maybe I am just hungry?

'What about the nice man and woman,' I say to her finally. 'Do you think we could go and visit them?'

'What a great idea,' she smiles. 'Let's go.'

And so we spring together up the steps, across the street, down one of the alleys and run up, up away from the harbour. We get to a dusty track and walk down it. I notice some of the dust has covered Lilette's lovely white fur on her belly.

'You need a clean,' I say to her, smiling.

'Oh, don't worry about that,' she answers. 'Just wait till we get there.'

---

[44] Towards the end of 1948, the Amethyst took part in a regatta in Hong Kong.

We reach a house that has a fence outside. Lilette squeezes through a gap and I follow her. I don't think Peggy would have been able to squeeze through. It is very tiny. Even I only just about make it. We are on a small patch of grass and I sniff. It smells of birds and flowers. I can't smell any other me's or dogs or anything else though.

'Do you like this garden?' Lilette asks as I stand there, taking it all in.

'Yes. It still doesn't look very much like the sea though.' She looks at me puzzled as I continue to sniff. A small black thing appears from nowhere and flies around my head. It tries to land on my nose so I shake my head. It makes a funny buzzing sound and I try to jump up and catch it.

'What are you doing?' Lilette purrs at me. 'Haven't you seen a fly before?'

So, that's what they're called. As well as what they do. She mewls as we reach a door. It opens and a human looks down at us both.

'Hello, hello, where have you been?' the woman says. 'And my, who's this?'

I lift my tail up and let myself be stroked by her. She is wearing a very pretty dress and smells even more like the flowers than the flowers do.

Lilette and I both follow the woman. We pad across a tiled floor and the woman places two bowls in front of us and fills them with food. It is nice, but not as nice as the magic food in the tin from the Captain or from the shop owner. I eat it anyway. Shall I leave some or shall I eat it all? If I was on the ship then I know I could leave some, but here, I don't think so, so I eat it all. Even though I know I like being on the ship, I like places like this. Places where I can get fed and then just explore if I feel brave and if I want to. Peggy says she much prefers to be fed by just one human and follow them around, but I don't, I prefer the opposite. That word again.

When we have both finished eating and the woman has given us some water to drink, a man comes in. He picks Lilette up. I think she might go to scratch him, but she doesn't. She lets him take her through to another room. I follow and watch. The woman is behind me. The man has a very small broom with him, more small than the ones the sailors use back on the ship. Is he going to try and make Lilette and me do some cleaning? I thought only women used big ones to clean the outside of their homes. Oh, and the men on the ship use them too of course. Ah, I see now. He strokes Lilette's back with it and brushes and brushes and brushes her so she is very clean. Her fur all fluffs up as he brushes the

106

dust away from her belly. He even cleans her paws with a cloth. I think I would sneeze and pull them away if someone tried to do that to me.

At last the man stops brushing Lilette.

'There you go. Look at you now.'

Lilette drops down from his knees. She looks lovely.

'What about you?' the man says to me. 'Do you want to have a nice brush too?'

I stand there and stare at him. I don't really want to go over.

Lilette stares at me. 'Go on,' she nods. 'Haven't you ever been brushed before?'

No, I haven't. I like to clean myself. I don't know if I would like a human to do it for me. Do humans clean each other, I wonder.

The woman looks down at me and smiles. 'It does feel marvellous.' Perhaps humans do brush each other then... How odd.

And so I creep slow over to the man. He pats his knee. I look over at Lilette again and then jump up on him. I can feel his hand on my back and then it feels as if I am trying to run under something because it scrapes all along. Do I like this? No, not at first. It hurts. He must brush over my... scattle bars, as Peggy calls them, because it stings. Then the man must see them because he says, 'Ouch, oh poor little thing. Who did that to you?'

He stops brushing my back and does my belly instead. Then he brushes my front and back legs. Sometimes, he has to brush quite hard and pull. 'You've got a few clumps in here,' he says. 'Have you fallen in the sea?' I can see some of my hairs in the brush. I hope he doesn't brush me away completely.

He gives my head a little brush and I can feel all my fur spring up. I think I prefer cleaning myself to be honest, but I want to look brave in front of Lilette.

'There you go,' the man says after a while and puts the brush down. 'Looks like you've been in the wars a little, but you're all shipshape now.'

I might not know what the wars are, but I know I am not the shape of a ship.

I feel all light. All clean and fluffy. I hope I look as good as Lilette.

We trot through the house, on tiles and on what feels like fur, until we reach a door. Lilette mewls. The woman has been following us. 'So, you want to go back outside? OK then,' and she opens the door and lets us both out.

We run across the garden, squeeze through the gap and out along the track. It is more dark now, but the stars are out. We run round a corner and get to a part that overlooks the harbour. I can see all the ships. I think I can even see the Amethyst. I recognise the lifeboats at the back and the flag deck. I point it out to Lilette.

'That's mine,' I say to her. 'That's where I live.'

'Tell me another story,' she whispers and nuzzles up to me. I feel, what was it Peggy said? As if I had been eating butterflies? No, I feel much more good than that.

And so I tell her about playing with the die. About the brown drink and the Captain who is ill. More stories about the rats and what I must do to them.

'You are very brave,' she says to me. 'I haven't been anywhere except this place.'

'But you like it here though, don't you?' I ask her.

'Oh yes. I like the humans who feed me and look after me. I don't know if I would want to be anywhere else.'

That's what I used to think, I think.

We sit there and carry on looking down at the ships below and at the stars up above. There are more stars now, twinkling down. Lilette's eyes gleam. She tells me about the best places to chase mouses, a shop that gives her food sometimes and how she doesn't like the bang, bangs, even if it does mean there are lots of stunned fish to eat.

My head spins all the time as I listen to her. Her scent is all around me. It seems to get more strong and more strong. Then she leaps up and runs back down the track fast, fast. Spinning around and jumping behind trees. I spring over her, around her. We laugh and smile a lot. I wish we had played together a lot more before George had found me. I wish I had been more brave.

Then, as the sky is most dark, dark and the stars seem to get even more bright, we go down a small alley that is full of boxes and crates.

Now, I'm not sure what game it was we played in the alley, but when I came out, I didn't feel as if I wanted to run and jump about and scratch things as much. I still felt good though, much better than I have ever felt before. In fact, all I am going to mention about it is that, when I *did* finally come out of the alley, let's just say I was a much, much happier, older and smarter cat than when I went in...

****

It is almost bright when I get back to the Amethyst. On the way back I come across a small, stopped bird, so I pick it up, thinking that George might quite like it. Welburn, the bosun's mate, sees me as I trot along the dock. He very kindly puts the tongue out so I can run back up.

'Here, Simon,' Welburn calls as I skip across the deck. 'You look like the cat who's had the cream.'

What does he mean? Or maybe he knows? How does he know? Do I look different? I certainly feel very different. I slink off.

'What's the matter,' he calls after me. 'Cat got your tongue?'

I know where my tongue is. And the ship's tongue. Why do humans make sense sometimes and then other times they make no sense at all? If us... cats... ruled the world I'm sure it would be a much finer place. I slip on the deck as I run across it. Some sailors are out on deck and they are scrubbing and scrubbing. I skip all along the port side, reach the big chain and go into the doorway, heading for the stowage. I pad in and spy Peggy's box. Should I jump on her or just give her a lick? I go over to the box and put my head in. Peggy isn't there. That's strange. I know she is usually asleep here, especially when it stops being dark and starts to get light again.

I run around to the stern. No sign of her or her business. There are a few crumbs of food and a slight smell of the rats. As I run up the starboard side I can smell the rats more and more, but can't see any though. I get to the bridge, put my head in to see if she is in there, then scamper up to the bow. I even look all round and behind the turrets. Peggy is nowhere to be found. I see Welburn standing next to the ship's tongue. How I wish I could ask him where Peggy is.

I think I see a dark shape run quickly past. That can't have been Peggy. Too small and much too fast. I try to follow the shape to see where it ran off to, but it has gone now. I get to another doorway. Shall I go to the lower deck or down here? I decide to go to the lower deck. Maybe Peggy is sleeping near George, waiting for me to come back? In the mess room I hear snoring and see boots and bodies. I can smell them too. I even run right down, down to a room where me, Peggy and only some of the sailors are allowed. I don't know why everyone can't go in though. When I get there it smells very bad indeed. The air is thick and hot; it doesn't smell right at all. There are lots of sailors in here snoozing and coughing. What is going on?

I go to the stores, but they are closed so I run through the galley, but no one is in there either. Where is she? I go back to the doorway and jump down the stairs. Down here leads to the engine room. Me and Peggy do not come down here because we always get shooed away. Besides, when the ship is moving, this is the hottest room. The sailors who work in here are always busy, busy and they just shout at us to get out.

But there are no sailors in here now. It is not so hot and a lot quieter. I run around and have a little sniff. I am just about to leave when I hear a small whimper. I run right to the back of the engine room. There, hiding behind a pipe, is Peggy. She looks more sad than I have ever seen anyone. Even more sad than when George's eyes are wet. I drop the bird.

'Peggy, Peggy. It's me. What's wrong?'

Her head is buried in her paws and her ears are right, right down. She moves a paw away from her face and stares up at me. Big, brown, wet, sad eyes.

'Oh, Simon.'

'What? What is it?' I want to know. I squeeze in next to her and she shuffles over a little. 'Lots of the sailors are ill,' she sniffles. 'Some of them have to sleep away from the others for a while. But some of them have been taken away. And the Captain... he's gone.'

Gone. Not that word again.

'The Doctor came and said the Captain should go with him.[45] So they've both left. He won't be coming back,' and Peggy cries again.

So, not gone, but not on this ship anymore. It is still very sad though. Sad for me. Sad for Peggy. And the sailors as well, I suppose. Who will be the Captain now? Who will play the die game with me? Whose hat will I sleep in?

'He rescued me and looked after me. Who will do that now?' she whimpers.

'Oh, Peggy. You have me. We will look after each other. The sailors will still feed us.'

She looks up. 'I wish I could have said goodbye. I wish I could have licked his hand. It was all very quick.'

So do I, I think. I could have chased after the die. I could have picked it up and run away with it so he would come and find me instead of leaving the ship. I was happy before; now I feel sad again. Funny how things can change so quickly.

'Why do people have to go?' she asks. 'I don't like change.'

---

[45] Captain Griffiths was not very sick - although many sailors were - but left the ship to take command of a different vessel. He contracted poliomyelitis in 1949 and died in January of that year.

'But it changed when I came here,' I mewl.

'Yes, but that change was good. This is bad.'

I don't know what to do. Or what to say. What will make Peggy feel happier?

'What do you need?' I say to her. 'Do you need a lick?' She nods her head and gives a little smile. I lick her wet nose. 'Do you need some food?' I ask her. Her smile is bigger, her head more noddier. She looks at my bird.

'You're not having that,' I say to her. 'That's for George.'

I run out of the engine room, up the stairs, through the doorway, round and out onto the deck. I don't quite know where I am going to get some food from, but I will find some. Anything to make Peggy feel more like herself. I run up the port side again and scamper up to the bow. I am just about to go up to the bridge when I spy, not Welburn, but Mao Tse Tung. Rats are running up the tongue one at a time. He squeaks something to them and they run off starboard. Here's another one. And another. They scurry right across the deck of the ship. *Our* ship.

I shrink back. Oh no. This is too much. This is too bad. Peggy was right and I was wrong. We have been feeding them, helping them so they won't make my friends ill and now there are more and more of them coming on board. Mao Tse Tung must have told them how easy it is to live on this ship. To be fed by a cat and a dog instead of being chased by them. Chased and caught by *me*.

I feel... the opposite of how I felt when I was with Lilette. I don't want the rats to see me. Not just yet. I don't want to be seen and I don't want to feel like this. I want to be a happy cat again. I want Peggy to be a happy dog too. How can I tell her what I have just seen? She will be more sad than ever. I find myself in the lower deck, squeeze through all the swinging beds and jump up on George. His eyes meet mine.

'Where've you been?' he asks. 'I thought you were never going to come back. And what's that you've got?'

I mewl and drop the bird on him.

'Er. Thanks.' George picks it off himself - I can tell he likes it - and drops it on the floor. He picks up a small bag next to his present. 'And I have something for you and Peggy. Well, from the Captain. Jimmy was helping him to pack. He said the Captain even managed a smile when Jimmy found whatever it was of Peggy's. He put something in there for you too.'

George places the bag on his chest in front of me. I stick my nose in and it rustles a little. I can't smell anything. Wait! Actually I can now. Something familiar. George puts his hand in and brings out a small... it's the die. The Captain's die! He left it for me. George puts his hand in the bag again and pulls out a… what is it? It's an old chewed sock, with a bit on the top that looks like it has been ripped off. Oh, I know what this is. I didn't understand what George and Conway were shouting to each other about socks but I do know this is an old, blue, smelly sock.

No, it isn't! It's got an ear. It must be Peggy's smelly old sock toy monkey. I might not know what a monkey is, but by the look of this one I really hope I do one day because they look cute and lovely. And I know this smell of course and I know exactly who it belongs to. What did I say about wanting to make Peggy happy again?

I leap off the bed and run, run, run back down to the engine room.

'Hey!' George calls after me.

15/ Say *fromage*

All around is blue. A slightly different blue than what I have seen before, but still blue. George says it's because we are on the South China Sea like before, but here it is much deeper, so even though the water seems the same, it is a lot darker too. Funny. We have been out on the sea for a long time, sometimes stopping, sometimes not.[46] We have been to a place called Port Dickson in Malaya and picked up some humans that George said were called the Malay Regiment. Port Dickson was quite small. The humans were too.

They didn't sail with us for long, but they made the sailors laugh because of how they used the heads.[47] I still don't know why they call them that. George said the humans from Malay would squat with their feet on the seat instead of sitting down and they would fall off when the sea was rough and make a mess. When George told me that, at first I thought he meant they would have their heads on the floor and their legs in the air, but how funny that different humans do their condodderate business in different ways too, and that they can get into trouble if they do it wrong.

Now George says we are heading north this time, instead of south. I know what north and south mean; they mean up and down like

---

[46] Between November 1948 and before the Amethyst's 'Yangtze Incident' in April 1949, the ship was on patrol duty on Malayan waters and sailed to and from Shanghai.

[47] Navy slang for toilets.

east means starboard and west means port, but I don't know how he can tell that we are moving north instead of south. Over there is the sea, behind us is the sea. All around: the sea. When it is daytime I know that the sun appears on our starboard side and on the port side when it is sleep time for the sailors. At night time George points out the moon and the stars and says sailors used to look at the moon, the stars and the sun to navigate. I just feel the hot sun burning me and see the stars twinkling and the moon that sometimes follows the ship and other times when it is not there at all.

And as well as the blue being all around, the funny thing is that Peggy says both of us have the blues too. Having the blues means we are very sad. Does that mean the sea is always sad then? Or the sky? And when they change colour does that mean they aren't sad anymore? I don't know. I don't know what to feel or think lately. When I close my eyes to go to sleep I sometimes get scared. I don't see many pictures of JoJo anymore and that makes me unhappy. I do see pictures of Lilette, but a lot of the time we are both being chased and I don't know what by. I think it is a monster, but I never actually see one. So that is why I am sad. I miss JoJo. I miss Lilette. And also I am sad because of those rats. The horrible, smelly bad rats.

Peggy is still a little unhappy because she misses the Captain, although she was very happy when I surprised her with her old toy monkey. Funny how dogs can be sad, but then suddenly change when they smell food or an old, soft toy.

I miss the Captain as well. I miss his hat, but at least I have George. The Captain brought Peggy on board so she is sad because she was not able to lick him goodbye. We have a new Captain though. He was the man I saw talking to Jimmy when we stopped in Hong Kong. His name is Skinner but he is still the Captain.[48] Another human with more than one name. Like Weston. Like me. The new Captain is smaller and fatter than the old one. He does not smile as much and the men don't laugh as much when he is around either. Peggy says he is very stern, but I don't think he looks that much like the back of the ship. He is here because the other Captain was too poorly to carry on. They sent him back to a place called England. Peggy said I would like it there, but that we will never get to go there because the ship lives here.

---

[48] Lieutenant Commander Bernard Skinner.

Like lots of the other sailors, the Captain was ill because of something called smallpox.[49] It isn't called smallpox because it has something to do with small humans, it is called that because it is very small, I suppose, so small that it cannot be seen. It makes humans very ill for a very long time. Peggy said she could tell lots of the sailors had it because they all came out in blotches. That meant they were also infectious. A strange word for a strange thing. It's a bit like the rats making sailors ill, but without the rats having to do anything, just be around, not even run over their food or anything. Because so many of the sailors had red blotches they had to sleep away from the other sailors who didn't.

And nobody could get off the ship either, apart from Peggy and me. We only went off once or twice though. Peggy didn't really want to and I didn't want to leave Peggy. I tried to look for Lilette, but each time I went back and ran through the port and tried to smell her I couldn't. I even went to look for the nice man and woman, but I got a bit lost and confused. Besides, I still wasn't quite sure that Chairman wouldn't be lurking around, ready to pounce. When all the sailors stopped getting red blotches on their faces we left Hong Kong. Now we are sailing to a place called Shanghai. I don't know why we are going there, but I'm sure it will be fun.

And all the while, Peggy and I have been trying to get rid of the rats. It is very hard though. There are so many of them. I think I can see them even when the sailors can't. A quick black flash just out of my sight, a scent near the stores as if they have been near there. I want to stop them, but I don't know how. I'm sure if we tried to trap them in Peggy's box again then they would just remember and run away. I bet I am not the only creature who learns, even if I haven't yet learnt of another plan that will stop them once and for all.

Stop, stop, stop. Gone, gone, gone. JoJo has gone, even if I do sometimes see him when my eyes are closed. Lilette, the Captain, even Uboat - gone, yet still around. Just somewhere else, in a different place. I still think it is funny that, for some things, there is just one word. JoJo gone is not the same as Uboat gone. The ship coming to a stop is not the same as when JoJo stopped. But I know what stopped means when it is to do with JoJo. I just find it very hard to think of it or to say it. It means

---

[49] Around the period in which this story is set, there was a smallpox outbreak on board the Amethyst, leading to several sailors being quarantined on board. Animals don't get smallpox so Simon and Peggy were fine.

died. JoJo died. And to make the rats be gone or stopped then I have to make them die. I have to kill them.

I am out on deck trying to lick behind my head and to see a picture of no rats, when a man in a very blue and very smart suit appears. I know what he is and even who he is. He is called a passenger. He isn't a sailor though. He is on this ship because he is important and he wants to go to where we are sailing. The name of this important passenger is Henri Cartier-Bresson.[50] He always carries something which hangs down around his neck. He puts it up to his face and it goes 'click, click, click.' Very different to when Peggy and me go 'clack, clack, clack.'

Henri sees me and comes over. '*Bonjour, le chat*,' Henri says and chuckles to himself.[51] I have heard him speak using lots and lots of words that I don't understand, but then he speaks in words that I do understand, even if it is quite funny when he says them. It's a bit like when I try to pretend I am like Peggy and use the same words that she does sometimes, only I can't do it. It hurts my throat. When Henri speaks it sounds almost as if he has eaten one of those yellow and black things that like flowers and give me a horrible bite if I go too near them.

George told me Henri is French, but I don't know why he said that because French is one of the sailors and Henri looks nothing like him.[52] I don't know why he would get them mixed up. Humans are so confusing at times.

Henri bends down and strokes me. The thing round his neck swings forward and hits me on my nose.

'*Désolé*,' he says and sits down on the deck next to me.[53] He reaches into his pocket. I wonder what he's got for me. Maybe it's food.

---

[50] Photographer credited as the father of photojournalism or reportage style photography. He travelled on board the Amethyst, possibly to head to Shanghai to document the Chinese uprising. The dialogue he has with Simon is paraphrasings of actual quotes that have been attributed to him.

[51] French for Hello, cat.

[52] Jack French, aged 22, a telegraphist on board HMS Amethyst.

[53] French for Sorry.

Hope so. He brings out something that looks like the things George wanted to post in Singapore. The time when the scary monsters with no names chased me. I sniff the edge of whatever it is he is holding. It is open at one end. I give it a lick and my mouth almost shuts together.

'Ha, ha,' says Henri, rubbing my head. ''Ere, let me.' He puts his hand inside and slides some pictures out. I look at them but I don't recognise the human in them. He looks a bit like some of the pictures that George has of ladies with very few clothes on and a bit like the man we saw cleaning his teeth in that horrible water. Maybe it is him?

'You see this man?' Henri points. 'You know this man?'

Of course I don't. He is a brown man, with very few clothes and with those things in front of his eyes that humans like to wear and I sometimes bite and run off with. Some of the sailors on this ship have them on their faces at times. The man in the picture has a nice face though. Peaceful. Like the sea out here.

'I...,' and Henri grabs the thing round his neck, presses the top of it, makes a clicking noise and points to the pictures he is holding, 'I take these.'

Take them? He can have them. They're his anyway, aren't they?

'This man,' Henri points again, 'Is Gandhi. I took these photos and was with 'im just one 'our before... ' and Henri moves his finger across his throat. So Henri was with this Gandhi man for an hour and stroked him? How nice of him. For both of them.

'I have photographed many famous people. King George the Sixth.'

I look at Henri. Does he mean my George? And six what? Six kings?

'Although you may know 'im as Albert,' Henri continues.

Now he is just confusing me again. Why do humans have more than one name sometimes?

Henri puts his face right up close to mine. 'I did not take any photographs of the king though. My subject. I only took photographs of 'is subjects instead,' and he throws his head back and laughs. 'But Gandhi was my subject and you can be my subject also. Come, come,' and Henri stands up. Before I even have a chance to follow him, or stand still, or run away, Henri has picked me up and tucked me under his arm. His thing hits me on the head again and now we are walking to the back of the ship.

We reach the stern and, as I scrabble with my back legs, he plonks me firmly on the floor. Henri puts his hand above his eyes, looks up, back at me, picks me up and plonks me the other way around.

Then he sticks one of his thumbs up.

He walks slowly bottomwards away from me, holding his thumb up and grabbing his thing with his other hand. He puts it to his face.

'*Maintenant. Assieds-toi.*'[54]

What? I sit down, confused.

'*Bon. Bon.*'[55] Then he clicks the thing and I am blinded by sunshine. He clicks again and I try to move away, although I can't really see. He comes right up close to my face, clicks and moves away from me. Why is he doing this? Why is he trying to make me not see?

'You know, *le chat*,' he says to me. 'It is an illusion that photos are made with the camera. They are made with the eye, the 'eart and the 'ead.'

Something about the eye?

Click. Click. Click.

'You like 'aving your photograph taken?' he asks me. Is that what he is doing? Taking something from me?

'Maybe you will get into photography too,' he laughs. 'Please remember though. Your first ten thousand photographs are your worst… '

I wish I could understand what he is talking about. I lie down and Henri starts clicking again.

'*Fantastique. Sois naturel.*[56] A photograph is neither taken nor seized by force. It offers itself up. It is the photo that takes *you*. One must not *take* photos,' and he jabs me with his finger, a little too hard for my liking.

---

[54] French for Now. Sit down.

[55] French for Good. Good.

[56] French for Fantastic. Act natural.

Next, he grabs me and we scramble up to the flag deck. I walk in and out amongst... this... and that.

'Stop,' he shouts.

Eh?'Stay still, *le chat*. Did you know that, of all the means of expression, photography is the only one that fixes a precise moment in time?'

No. I didn't know any of that. I only wish Peggy were here so she could explain to me exactly what is going on right now. If this has anything to do with pictures, then I'm sure she would love it.

'*Non, non*, what are you doing?'[57] Henri shouts at me again. 'You are thinking too much. Thinking should be done before and after photographing. Not during.'

I am getting a little bored of this now so I decide to run off. Down, down the stairs, round here and I'll just hide he— Oh no! Here he is again. Pointing and clicking. Go *away*!

'*Bon. Bon*,' Henri says again. 'To me, photography is the simultaneous recognition, in a fraction of a second, of the significance of an event.'

When is this ever going to *end*? I'm getting hungry now. Besides, I still have to think about what to do to get rid of the rats. I run off again. Henri hasn't finished with me yet though. He corners me under some stairs.

'That's right. Be creative,' and he puts his head right under the stairs. 'The creative act lasts but a brief moment, a lightning instant of give-and-take, just long enough for you to level the camera and to trap the fleeting prey in your little box.' Oh, so that's what he's done, is it? We'll see about that. As Henri messes with his thing, I squeeze between his legs and run, run right up to the bow.

'A photographer must always work with the greatest respect for 'is subject and in terms of 'is own point of view,' Henri shouts as he jumps up the stairs after me. I wish the old Captain was here. I could run fast into his cabin and hide under his hat. Instead, I just stand there, my blinded eyes gleaming, the wind in my fur. I must look terrible.

'Stay like that. Stand still,' Henri shouts again and thrashes his arms around wildly. 'As time passes by and you look at portraits, the people come back to you like a silent echo. A photograph is a vestige of a

---

[57] French for No, no.

face, a face in transit. Photography 'as something to do with death. It is a trace.' I try to move out of his way again. 'You must remember that. It's *très important.*'[58]

I hunch right back, ready to run around him, through his legs, jump right into the sea if I need to. He clicks again. 'Mwah,' he puts his fingers to his lips then flings his fingertips upwards as if he is pulling something out of his mouth. 'That was it. The decisive moment.[59] *Adorable.*' He bends and goes to... I don't know what with me... but I see my chance, jump up, on his back, down the other side and run, run, run. Anything to get away from this silly man with the silly clicky thing that is right in front of his face. What good would ever come of that? How strange and silly these humans are, even the ones that are supposed to be important.

---

[58] French for Very important.

[59] The phrase that Bresson coined to describe his style and approach.

16/ Nine of me

I can breathe now. Well, not really, because where we are is very... humid. Peggy told me that word. But I can breathe, safe in the knowledge I won't get chased around the ship again by Henri and his clicky thing. I think I would rather be the one doing the chasing than the one being chased, thank you very much. The ship went to Shanghai and he got off, so that's the end of him. I don't know what he was going to do there - chase lots of cats around and make their fur stand on end probably. When I told Peggy about it she said she wished she had not been asleep as she likes having her picture taken. I'm still not sure why she would be happy having her pictures taken away from her. She is a lot happier now that she has her monkey back than without it though.

I am on the mess deck with Peggy, her monkey and some of the sailors. She is lying under a table, chewing; the sailors are eating and I am licking. I think that now might be the right moment - the decisive moment - to tell Peggy about the rats. Now is all we have, after all.

I peer out from behind my back leg.

'Peggy,' I call over to her, but she is too busy munching.

'Peggy,' I hiss again. She looks up, spittle running from her mouth down onto her monkey's head. 'Mmm. What? What is it? Is it food time?' Both her ears prick up.

'No, but it's about the food. Sort of.'

The monkey's ear flops forward. As does one of Peggy's.

I pad over to her. 'Have you noticed that we are taking more and more food up to the stern?' I ask her.

'Not sure,' she replies. 'But we've been doing a lot more walking. Do you want a chew?'

'No thanks. Well, I think... No, in fact I *know* we have a lot more... what did you call me when George brought me on here?'

'I don't remember,' and she starts to annoy her monkey again. She is starting to annoy me too.

'Mao Tse Tung must have told some other rats about being fed all the time. There's... twenteen more rats than when I first came on board. Lots of them.'

'Are you sure, dear heart?' she answers.

'Yes. I think sometimes I can see them. Can't you smell them more?' I look around, almost expecting some rats to run through the mess deck right there and then.

'Well, we'll just have to put a stop to them this time, won't we?' Peggy answers. 'I might be many things, but one thing I most certainly am not is a soft touch.' A sailor drops some food under the table next to Peggy. Instantly, she rolls over, or tries to roll over, sticks her legs in the air and makes the most pathetic noise.

I know she is right. I wish I knew how to though.

Jimmy comes in with the Captain. 'Attention!' and all the sailors stop eating, stand up straight away and hit the side of their head with their starboard hand. Even I stand up. Peggy doesn't though; she just flops over again to one side. The Captain sees me, but he does not smile at me like the other one used to.

'We've just had an order come over the wireless,' the Captain says, looking back at the sailors. 'We have to move with Godspeed and head down to Nanking.'

'Why, sir?' Atkins pipes up.

'I'm coming to that, good lord,' the Captain says, quite angry.

'Some of our boys on the HMS Consort have run into some difficulty.[60] HMS London is on her way too.[61] Consort has come under fire from some of those blasted Chinese Communists—'

---

[60] C class destroyer of the Royal Navy. Launched in 1944 and scrapped in 1961. Whilst stationed near Nanking on the Yangtze River, the Consort came under fire from Chinese Communists. The Amethyst was sent to initially relieve and then provide support to the Consort.

[61] County class heavy cruiser of the Royal Navy. Launched in 1927 and scrapped in 1950.

Chinese Connunists? That's what the other Captain thought I was. I wonder if I am. I don't think so.

'Now, I don't need to remind you that we remain neutral in this particular darned skirmish, but we can't have any of our ships being fired on.'

Some of the sailors mutter something like, 'Hear, hear,' but I don't know why. I can hear the Captain quite well.

'ETA is nine hours.[62] The Nationalists are sending ships to escort us.[63] Jimmy will keep you informed as to any developments,' and he walks out.

All the sailors start talking and raising their voices after the Captain walks out. Shouts of, 'I thought we were heading back to Hong Kong,' and, 'What about shore leave?'

Jimmy raises his hand and the men all fall silent. 'Orders from above. Can't be helped. Some of those on the Consort have been away on commission for nearly three years, so think yourselves darned lucky.'

'Why are they being fired at?' George asks Jimmy.

'Don't know,' he answers. 'They all seem a bit trigger happy to me.'

'Will we get fired at?' George asks again.

'No, we darned won't,' Jimmy answers. 'We'll fly the White Ensign and the Union Flag on the jack staff and paint the Union Flag on the hull as well. That'll show 'em who we are. But, as a precautionary measure, we'll prepare some live ammunition. Besides, we've done our bit for this region; they can sort the rest of it out their darned selves. We stay out of it. All's fair in love and war and all that.'

Now I've heard of love and I know what that is. I heard the man who brushed Lilette and me say it too, but I still don't know what it

---

[62] Estimated Time of Arrival.

[63] The Chinese Civil War began in 1927 and ended in 1950, although the two warring factions united in 1937 to form a Second United Front to counter the Japanese invasion. The civil war was resumed in 1946. The war represented an ideological split between the Left Communist Party of China and the right Nationalists loyal to the Republic of China. The conflict eventually resulted in two de facto states, the Republic of China (ROC) in Taiwan and the People's Republic of China (PRC) in mainland China, both claiming to be the legitimate government of China.

means. But if war is the same as love and they are both fair, then that means everything is going to be all right. Good. I quite like the sound of this Nanking place too. I wonder why it is called that. Maybe it's because one of those kings lives there. I wonder how many there are of him and if he has more than one name too. Not long now until I find out, I suppose…

****

Later, I am lying on top of George. I have just finished taking food up onto the stern with Peggy. It is much harder now because she does not want to let go of her toy monkey since she has found it again. Sometimes I even have to pull it off her and drop it into her box in the stowage.

'No one will take it away from you again,' I mewl at her. I know how she feels about her toy though. The only thing I really used to play with all the time was JoJo and I know how much I miss him; his shape, his smell, his ears.

'We reach Nanking in the morning then,' George says, rubbing my head. I purr and stretch my claws out.

'Ow. Don't do that,' he chuckles, moving them away. Then he looks a little scared and worried.

'I do hope everything will be OK,' and he touches one of the pictures next to his swinging bed.

I know things will be OK though. I can sense it. From being a scared little me hiding and George finding me, coming here on this ship, meeting Peggy, the very nice Captain and the not very nice McCunnell, almost getting thrown overboard, being chased by monsters in Singapore, catching rats, playing with Lilette and doing… that… my one life so far has been wonderful. What did Peggy say? That there was good and bad in everyone, in everything. Since I came on board this ship there has been some bad, but there has been lots and lots of good as well. Everything is magic, Peggy is right. And I am right as well; everything is good and will carry on being good.

George rubs my head again. 'You're very lucky being a cat, you know.'

He's right as well. I am.

'They say that us humans only have one life—'

And so do I, I think.

'But you,' he continues. 'Well, they say cats have nine lives… '

Nine? That's more than six but less than twenteen. But nine? That's news to me. But if that's true, what happened to JoJo and his other

126

- whatever one less than nine is - lives? Maybe he has not gone after all and he is just somewhere else as well as just being in my pictures? No, he'd stopped. He'd gone. He was... dead. I like the picture of nine lives much more than the picture of dead. I purr as George continues to stroke me. The picture changes to nine JoJos and nine me's. Well, lots of us both, anyway.

'Guess what?' I run up to him and cuddle him. 'I have nine lives. Everything is good and magic.'

I can feel his heart, beating, beating...

17/ Action stations

'There I was in my box, with monkey by my side of course, when I was woken by the most dreadfully beastly sound. Louder than if all the dogs in the world decided to bark at the same time. It reminded me of when I used to live at home with my master and I would hear a horrible wailing that would rumble all around my belly. I'd have to run in from the garden and join the others all bunched up in the cellar. Even our maid was in there.

'Now, I'm used to hearing all the sailors shouting and running around - sometimes they even put their heads right into my box and shout, 'Peggy, Peggy,' - but this wailing was truly frightening and horrible. Frightfully horrid, you could say, if you could hear yourself above all the racket and commotion after someone shouted, 'Action stations!'

'Thankfully the noise on the ship didn't last long. The men were still most frightfully busy though. They even came into the stowage to collect some things, but goodness knows what. They must have speeded up the ship too for some reason because I heard the noise of the engine shift somewhat and I certainly felt a decided pull. Accustomed as I am to high jinks on the high seas, I settled back into my box ready for another snooze before I went off to help with those beastly rats.

'And then - whoosh! And a boom! It nearly knocked me right out of my box, it did. I stepped out of it to see what all the fuss and commotion was for and was just about to walk out onto the deck when lots of legs came rushing past me. They must have been eating their breakfast in the mess. I trotted out onto the deck just in time to hear someone bellow, 'Over there! Look out!'

'What on earth is happening? I thought, as I started to walk up the starboard side. 'Peggy! Get back!' I heard someone else shout, though lord knows who it was. The air was quite smoky and I saw some of the men unfurling Union Flags and hanging them over the side of the

boat. I trotted round to the other side of the ship and just about managed to get to the bow when 'Kaboom!!!'

'Oh, it was dreadful, it really was. Truly dreadful. 'Artillery fire. Over there,' I heard someone scream, but again I don't know who it was because the smoke was so thick I couldn't see a dicky bird. Someone's attacking us, I thought. And at this ungodly hour too. I haven't even had my breakfast yet.

'I decided to head up to the bridge - even though I know I'm not actually allowed in there, especially with this rather strict new Captain of ours. Then I heard more firing coming from the land I could just about make out and I saw a shell splash right across the bow. Let me tell you, I moved more quickly than I ever have before – faster even than when I was a puppy. I tried to run onto the bridge but, just as I managed to reach the door, there was another frightful whooshing sound and a terrible bang and clang as something knocked right into the side of the ship.

''Someone's firing at us,' I heard the Captain shout. 'Raise the battle and sign,' or some such rhubarb. And then there was that sound again. Even louder this time. Oh, my poor ears. I couldn't get away from that noise. I heard more firing, another whoosh and then it became dreadfully frightening because one side of the bridge just smashed in completely. Some of the men around me were immediately flung over and fell right onto the deck. They had blood all over their faces, in their hair, on their clothes. It was truly shocking. I was shaking all over, from my head right down to my tail.

'And then the smoke appeared. Gosh, how terrible that was. Thick and black and really stinging my eyes and my throat. And the smell, such an indescribable smell, one I've never smelt before and one I certainly don't want to ever have to smell again. I think it must have been coming from some of the men too because some of them were actually ablaze. My master used to tell me about shadows and monsters and I remember some of the things we saw at the cinema of course, but really, it was nothing, absolutely nothing compared to what was happening.

'I tried to peer through the smoke, but it really was most terribly thick. I kept stumbling over men all around me, some injured and screaming in pain, others that were definitely dead. I looked in the bridge again and could just make out Conway and the Captain lying on the floor. Welburn was at the wheel, but it looked as if he'd been hurt too. His face was covered in blood and I couldn't see his arm at all. As I watched, his body slid to the floor, knocked the wheel and I felt the whole ship lurch port side.

'I managed to get away from there, although goodness knows how because my back legs seemed to have given way. I had to keep *stepping over bodies and I really couldn't see anything. The smoke really was the most dreadfully awful thing. Some of the sailors were burning, actually burning. There was fire everywhere and that smell again. The worst stench I have ever had the misfortune to smell. I don't think I shall ever forget it. I crawled into a gap just under the stairs and squeezed myself into it. I could just about make out what was happening around me and I felt slightly safer in my hiding place, although I was trembling all over. I was grateful I couldn't see the land because that meant whoever was attacking us couldn't see me. I always thought I wanted to be a much bigger dog, but I was awfully thankful of my size at that moment.*

'From my hiding place, I could see four sailors at the turrets on the bow trying to fire back at whoever was attacking us, but I don't think it was any use. Some of the sailors on the starboard side were trying to fire as well, but as soon as there was that whooshing sound again they just fell backwards and the firing stopped. And then I heard screaming. 'Help me. Over here.' The cries for help are still ringing in my ears now, but at the time I couldn't make out where that particular cry was coming from. Through the smoke I could see bodies lying on the deck, lots of blood, but I couldn't tell who was shouting and who wasn't. Nervously, I ventured out from my hiding place to lick the face of the sailor lying nearby, but he didn't move and I just knew he was dead.

'There was still lots of firing coming from the land. Through all the smoke I saw a sailor struggle to his feet, but something whizzed through the air, hit him in the face and he stumbled forward, almost landing right on top of me. It was truly terrifying - the smell, the sound of people screaming and that 'rat-a-tat' noise coming at us, seemingly from everywhere. Some of the sailors were trying to fire back with the ship's guns, but they were just falling on the deck instead, right in front of me. Everything was flying everywhere. When was this ever going to end?

'How I wished I could have seen properly through the smoke. I didn't know where anyone was anymore. I could have run right past my own master and not even noticed him; there was so much smoke, panic and commotion. I hoped and prayed everyone else was safe or hiding, I truly did. I didn't like the thought of anyone being dead, it was absolutely terrible witnessing what was happening to the sailors and God knows I know exactly what it's like when someone you love is not there anymore.

'I don't think the ship was hit again after that, not by the shells that made that dreadful whooshing sound anyway, though whoever was attacking us was still shooting at us. I heard pinging as the ship was hit, rather like the sound my paws make on here but much louder and much more frightening. I didn't know where they would come from next. Most, if not all, of the men were lying on the decks now. The ones who weren't

dead were crawling, trying to avoid being hit. They must have had to crawl over the bodies of some of their friends. How truly dreadful.

'Then the ship juddered to a halt with a massive crunch. I thought we must have hit something, but we must have lurched port side all the way into shallower waters. With no one at the wheel and the Captain dead there was no one to steer the ship, so it just drifted until it ran aground. There was still smoke everywhere and the dreadful smell still lingered, but then the firing stopped too. After all that commotion, the only sounds I heard were the haunting moans and groans of the men and the creaking of the battered ship.

'I don't know who it was who managed to slowly stand up first. I think it must have been First Lieutenant Weston because I heard him shout, 'Name and status,' and then I heard some of the men calling and shouting over each other. 'Conway: left leg.' 'Wills: dead.' 'Thomson: fingers and toes.'

''All bodies below deck,' Weston shouted again and all the men who were able walked, crawled or dragged themselves into a doorway. Some of them were helping others; some of them were trying to move their friends who weren't moving at all as the thick smoke hung around us and over the ship. There was lots of coughing and spitting as the men slowly came to.

'I grabbed a leg, I don't know whose it was, they were far too covered in blood for me to recognise, but I managed to give them a quick tug and they lifted their head up, got off the deck and tumbled down the stairs. Whoever it was said, 'Thanks Peggy,' and rubbed my head. Everyone was trying to escape from the smoke and the smell, but it wasn't much better on the lower decks. There were dead bodies and injured sailors down there too. The whole thing was a frightful mess.

''Right,' Weston called to the men who were down there. 'This situation is impossible, so we need to evacuate as soon as. They may have blasted a hole in the hull for all we know and we're at risk of sinking. Those of you who are able, look for any holes and plug the damned things up with hammocks, bedding, anything. You,' he pointed to Ginger, 'All the secret publications need to be burnt and the crypto equipment broken up into pieces. We're not letting whichever swines did this get hold of any of that.'

'Ginger went off. I presume he went to the ops room to start to get rid of things. We can't let our enemies get their hands on good old British secrets and equipment, heavens no.

''We need to shut the engines down too,' Weston commanded again.

"But if we do that we'll only have the emergency transmitter and receiver,' I heard someone say.

"Well what does that darned matter if she's going down anyway? Did we manage to send the distress signal out?'

"Yes, one was sent out. 'Under heavy fire. Am aground. Large number of casualties.'[64]

"Good. Well, at least that message got out,' Weston snapped. 'They'll be sending a ship up no doubt. Think HMS London is near the mouth of the Yangtze. And how about the doctor and sick berth attendant? Are they accounted for?'

"I'll go and check,' a sailor with a bloodied face shouted back and off he went. I remember my master telling me something about bulldog spirit and this is what he must have meant, although I've never been particularly fond of bulldogs myself.

"How many men have we lost?' a trembling voice asked.

"I don't know,' Weston bellowed. 'I expect the casualties are pretty heavy. I'll do a tally as soon as I can. Right, who's with me to get some of our men ashore?'

'There was a flurry of hands and activity then and all but the most badly injured went back outside on deck. I followed them up there, keeping my head as low down as possible. I really hoped we weren't going to get fired at again. Some of the men started to pull on ropes on the side of the ship and they managed to lower one of the boats into the water.

"Walking wounded in here,' Weston cried. 'Let's get them to the other shore. The Nationalists will be there. Although fat lot of darned use their ships were.'

"I think it was too narrow,' Gurns said. Oh, thank heavens Gurns was still alive and all in one piece.

"Too narrow, pah!' Weston growled. 'Clear the mess for the most injured,' he shouted at Gurns. 'When they send a ship up, they can take them to hospital. The rest of you, I hope you've got your water wings because you're going to have to swim for it.'

'I stuck my head out through the railing and could just about see the water below. It was a horrid black colour and was quite a far drop too. How was I going to get off? I'm ashamed to say I started to panic a

---

[64] Part of the actual message that was sent out.

little then. Before, it was scary but so frightening all I was doing was just concentrating on not being hit by anything. As it was, I had burnt my paws and my fur but, heavens, at least I wasn't like some of those poor old sailors that were still lying all around me.

'Then I saw some of the men stand up and crawl and somehow manage to make their way over to the men who were holding the ropes of the boat. They carefully and slowly helped all the wounded into the boat; some were even carried on. I don't quite know precisely how many men got into the boat, but I was glad to see that it was quite a few, let me tell you.

'As the boat was filling up, some of the other men swung their legs over the railing, stood on the gunwale and dropped into the water ready to swim to the relative safety of the shore. But then, oh heavens, it was terrible. As soon as the men dropped into the dark water they started to shout and scream. 'Help! Help! Oil. I can't swim in it!' I don't know what was happening to them; it looked as if they were being dragged down right underneath the water. Some of them had black all over their heads. They were trying to lift their arms out of the water and swim away from all the oil but they couldn't do it. It was dreadful.[65]

'Someone - I don't know who - pushed some of the other men away from the gunwale. 'Stop!' he shouted. 'Move up there. Look for patches where there's less oil and just swim for it.' I don't know where the men could have jumped in though, because everywhere I looked there were those damned beastly dark patches. The smoke was still lingering too; all I could see was black and blue. Some of the men must have found a better spot though, because I heard someone cry, 'Over here,' and I watched the men a bit further up the ship jump right in. I was relieved to see them swimming away from the ship towards the land. I could just about make it out. It seemed quite far to me, but I could tell some of the men were good swimmers so I just hoped they would make it.

'Then, oh heavens, that 'rat-a-tat' noise started up again and it seemed as if it had suddenly started to rain really heavily because there was that dreadful noise followed by splashes on the water's surface and awfully near the men's poor heads.

''Swim! Swim!' I heard someone shout. 'Underwater if you can.'

'And that's when I really started to panic, because I realised that whoever had attacked us was now actually shooting at the men in the

---

[65] Reports of oil in the water have been disputed.

134

water. Those who were in the boat tried to row over to rescue them and protect them, but it was no use. The sight of the men being hit and the screaming before their heads disappeared under the water was shocking, absolutely shocking. Truly awful. The splashing even made some of the oil in the water catch alight as the men were trying to swim through it and some of them just burnt and went under. Horrid. Absolutely horrid. And the screams again. I shall never forget them. Never.

'I watched the men in the boat slowly make their way over to the other shore. It was full of bodies, some of them moving, but some of them just lying very still. Men were still swimming in the water too. I could see their arms and heads, but some of the others who were surrounded by that frightful oil didn't make it. And all the while they were still being fired at. Shots hitting the water, hitting the men, hitting the ship.

'When are they going to stop firing? I thought. This is truly outrageous. Despicable behaviour. There weren't many of us left on the ship now. There were some on the deck not moving and those who could move or be moved were downstairs. Thankfully, those who didn't have too much blood on them were able to wrap things round the arms or legs of the others who had been hit. I hoped most of those in the boat and in the water had managed to get over to the other side, but then what was going to happen to us all next?

'I went back down to the lower decks. There was blood everywhere down there and men lying on the floor or just sitting there rubbing their heads. The look on their faces, they all looked the most terribly ghostly white colour. I went up to some of them and sat by them and tried to give them a lick. Some of them seemed to like it, but others didn't even seem to notice I was there. I saw McCunnell sitting on the floor, looking at his hands and just staring and staring.

'Gurns was tending to some of the sailors and making sure they were OK. Well, as OK as could possibly be expected anyway. He was rushing around, helping to stop the blood gushing from their heads or arms or giving people water to drink. Everybody must have breathed in some of that terrible stench, that dreadful smoke, because there were still lots of coughing and groaning sounds and I didn't feel too clever myself. All my insides were burning from swallowing that beastly smoke. Then, oh heavens above, I saw George sitting on the floor in the corner. He was rubbing his face and didn't seem to know where he was, so I wandered over and sat down next to him.

'He stroked my head and we sat there and watched what was going on. Then, very, very slowly, he stood up, using one hand to steady himself against the side of the ship. 'I need to make sure everyone's all right,' George said to me and he went to head out. I really didn't want to leave him, but I really didn't want to go back out on deck particularly either, but I thought it may be best if I just followed him. So out we went again, stepping over some of the men who were sitting on the floor and up the stairs.

'As we reached the deck I really wished I could tell him to keep his head down, but luckily all that dreadful firing seemed to have stopped. I was able to look down into the water, but I couldn't see anything apart from dark patches of that terrible oil. We crept along very slowly. There was still lots of dark smoke hanging in the air, but I think it was clearing a little. The dreadful stench was still there too. The whole ship was in an awful state. Red patches here, black patches there, bits of ship, sailors' boots, everything was all over the place.

'Luckily, George did keep his head down as we crept along the port side. I kept thinking at any moment he would get fired at and would just drop to the floor, then what would I have done? I saw some of the sailors collecting flags and hammocks and going below deck again. I really hoped they could fill up any holes. I didn't want the ship to sink, certainly not with all of us still on board it anyway.

'We moved very slowly, George kicking things out of the way so as to clear a path for me. We got to the bridge, or at least what was left of the bridge anyway. It was completely smashed to pieces. There's an awful lot of clearing up to be done, I thought when I saw all the mess. That's going to take such an awfully long time.

'And as George and I picked our way through all the bits of ship, we got to the bow and there, when we looked down, lying underneath a whole heap of goodness knows what, my heart nearly jumped out of my throat because that's when we found... you.'

18/ Aftermath

I don't know what is real and what is not real. JoJo is here and then he goes away again. I try to call out to him, but he just goes, goes, goes. I want to be cuddled up with him again. I don't want to be here. I don't even know where here is anymore. I don't want to feel like this. Something bad has happened and I feel bad. Really bad. Everything is bad. My ears are still screaming, as if all the monsters from Singapore are in my head, running around.

Peggy is breathless. She has told me the story about what happened. My head hurts. Everything hurts. I see her face and then the faces of monsters, of sailors covered in red, of Chairman. Did I really see him? His glinting green eye? Why was someone doing that to us? Peggy said there is good and bad everywhere, in everyone. Where is the good now? Peggy tries to give me a lick, but it stings too much when she does. I just want to lie here, wherever here is.

'Where is George now?' I ask her, my throat dry and sore.

'He's looking after some of the others,' she answers. 'Oh, Simon, it was truly awful, honestly it was. And you look awful too, if you don't mind my saying so. Much worse than in Singapore.'

I try to blink, but it is very hard. Wherever I am smells horrible, but then I realise the smell is coming from me. I try to move my head, to peer round and look at my back. Maybe I could give myself a clean? Ouch. Ow. No, it hurts too much.

'Don't move,' Peggy says quietly. 'Some of your fur has been singed and it looks like you're still covered in blood too. The doctor had to take bits of metal out from you, you know, and even stitch you back together,' and she shivers. 'They thought you were... ' but she stops.

Does she mean I nearly *stopped*?

'Are we still on the ship?' I ask her, looking around as best I can.

'Yes, we're in one of the store rooms right down below. Can't you see the others?'

I try to lift my head up again, but I can't really make anything out. The smell of... burnt... seems to be coming from everywhere, not just from me. I try to close my eyes again.

'Hey, Simon,' I hear a voice. George. 'My, my,' and I feel the touch of his hand, but shrink back.

'Sorry. Oh, you poor thing. Your back. We thought we'd lost you, you know... '

No, I wasn't lost. I was just... not here for a while. Did I really come close to... what happened to JoJo? If I felt like I was asleep and now I have woken up in all this pain in this... waking nightmare... then I must have done. Then, a sudden commotion. I hear the sound of feet running and someone bursting in.

'They've sent a rescue party! The HMS Consort.'

I hear some of the sailors groaning. 'Good, they can get us off this damned thing.'

'I'd best get upstairs,' George's voice. 'Peggy, d'you want to come too or stay here with Simon?'

I open my eyes and peer down at Peggy. She looks up at George. Then at me. Even though I am hurting all over and I cannot really move, I want to see everything for myself. I want to be there for George. I want to see the ship that is coming to rescue us. I whisper to Peggy, 'I want to see,' and I try to sit up.

'Here, no moving for you just yet,' George orders. 'But here,' and he wraps me in the blanket I am lying on and very slowly, carefully, lifts me up. 'Come on, tiger.'

Tiger?

We leave the horrible smell and the poor sailors in the room, go through a doorway and make our way up and out onto the deck. Down with the other sailors it was very dark, so it makes my eyes hurt when we get into the bright of outside. I feel like I did when George first brought me on here. Safe in his arms. There is a different smell out here. It does not smell of the sea. It smells, it smells like the engine room. I can see lots of red, the deck smashed, and broken parts of the ship lying here, there, everywhere. I look down and see Peggy gingerly stepping over... I don't know what they are.

I see sailors moving other sailors who are... not moving, placing them next to each other and covering them over. All lined up like whenever they leave the ship, but this time lying down instead of standing all straight. Some of the sailors who are doing the moving are drinking what looks like the brown liquid that our first Captain used to like. They don't look happy though. Not like when the Captain used to be drinking it. Other sailors are throwing things into the water. It takes a few of them to lift anything heavy, carry it and throw it over the side. Why are they doing that?

In the distance, I see a ship coming towards us, a bit like ours but with a much higher mast. There is lots of black smoke steaming out from the top of it. I look up and see flashes of light coming from our ship. The HMS Consort flashes back. It's as if they're speaking, but without words.

Some of the sailors standing near me are waving their hands in the air. They are smiling, but they don't look happy either. Their eyes seem to be staring at something else far away. George must see the Captain because I hear him shout, 'Sir,' and, for a moment, he takes one of his arms away from under me.

The Captain looks ill. Even more ill than the first one. He is all bent over and he keeps rubbing his head. 'The cavalry are here,' he says to George, Peggy and me as we reach him and he points to the Consort. Peggy looks up at me, her eyes a little brighter. 'I thought the Captain was dead. He doesn't look in too fine a form though.'

We stand there and watch as the Consort makes its way towards us, fast, but it still looks like it is some way away from us.

'She's travelling at a fair old speed, that one, sir,' George remarks to the Captain.

'Yes,' the Captain coughs and staggers as if his legs are as wibbly wobbly as mine.

'Looks like she's doing twenty-nine knots,' says Weston. 'Not close enough yet though for my liking. Their commander wanted to tow us out, but I'm not having any of it. We've signalled to them saying they'd be an easy target. How're we doing?' he asks a sailor as he rushes past.

'Plugging the damage as best we can, sir,' he answers. 'Don't think we'll be going down just yet.'

'Good, good,' Weston replies. 'And excess weight?'

'Anything that isn't fastened down is going over, sir. She's suffered a fair old amount of damage.'

'Yes. Yes I can see that. Keep me updated as to prog—'

Suddenly, he is interrupted by the Captain coughing and spluttering again, falling to his knees. He puts one hand forward to try and catch himself as he stumbles, but he collapses right in front of us on the deck.

I don't like this at all. I try to curl myself up into a small ball under George's arm. Peggy whimpers.

'Over here!' George calls to someone. 'Get him below deck.' A sailor, his face covered in red and his clothes black and torn comes rushing over. He bends, heaves the Captain over his shoulder and makes for the stairs. He slips as he does so; the deck is still covered in dark patches of... I don't know what.

The Consort is getting closer. Not long now before we are all rescued and safe, even more safe than here under George's arm. George puts his hand above his eyes to get a better look. Peggy gives a little wag of her tail. I can see one, two, three flags on it as it gets closer, the same as we have on here. Then I see even more - one, two, three, five, four, six, seven. I've done it.

'Good old Blighty,' Peggy barks proudly. At that moment, there is a 'crack, crack, crack' and the huge, scary flies appear again and whizz right over George's head. I hear Peggy howl, 'No! Not again!' and she runs off.

'Get down!' someone shouts. 'Hit the deck!'

Whizz! Crack! Now I try and make myself really small. George throws himself on the deck. I feel us falling forward and down. I see other sailors throw themselves on the floor next to us too or try and jump down the stairs.

'They're firing at us again,' George shouts above the noise. 'Simon. Are you all right?'

No. I'm not all right. I am scared, scared, scared. I don't like these flies. I don't like George being on the floor and I don't know where Peggy has run off to. The flies are clanging above our heads as they hit the ship, others whizzing right over to the other side. I see someone run past us, hear a whizz cut the air and watch as they are flung sideways onto the deck. Red splatters out everywhere.

'Oh please, please don't let George be hit,' I think. 'Don't let anyone else be hit.' I hope Peggy is safe. George crawls forward, me under one arm, my back legs dragging across the deck. Ow. Ow. Ow! I am too hurt to move. Too scared too mewl.

We hide behind a turret.

And then the loud bangs start. Just as loud as before. Just as frightening. Above me starts to fill with smoke again. Whooshing and banging coming from over there, the place where I am sure I saw Chairman, and now it is coming from the opposite side too. It must be coming from the Consort. They must be firing back at whoever is doing it to us and them.

'Keep down, Simon,' I hear George's voice. He doesn't need to tell me what to do. Not again. The first time I was under his arm I was frightened. Now I am trembling, shaking, hurting. This is worse than the bad pictures I see. This is real. I can smell it and hear it. I can feel the ship as it gets hit by the flies. Where is Peggy?

The flies stop whizzing above our heads, but the loud bangs carry on. Bang! Bang! From one side and then the other. George stands up, very, very slowly. No, George! Don't do it. We half crawl, half run right round to the other side of the ship, away from the land, from where the flies and the huge bangs are coming from, round to the other side. I see the Consort sailing right up close to us, smoke coming from the top of it and from the starboard side. The bangs stop as it sails past us. Wait! Wait! What did they say about rescue? George rescued me and brought me on here, now they have come to rescue us to get us all off. Why are they sailing past?

The Consort sails right past the stern of the Amethyst. More whizzes and bangs from where Chairman is. Where are they going? Why haven't they stopped?

'I think they must be turning round,' George whispers. 'There's no escape that way.'

The scary bangs stop as the Consort sails away. 'OK, let's get down below. See how everyone is,' George says and we rush downstairs. More sailors are covered in red. Gurns is there and, with him, Peggy.

'I'm frightfully sorry for dashing off Simon. I just couldn't face it all again. I don't know whether I'm coming or going.' She looks very sorry for herself. 'I think I might even have done my business up there. Not very considerate I know.' I sneeze a little and George must think I want to get down because he gently places me near Peggy.

Here we go. Ow. Ow! My back legs really hurt as I feel my paws touch the floor. I stand there, wobbling almost as much as Peggy's belly. I rock back and forth a little on my front and back legs. I try to move towards Peggy, but I can't do it. It isn't the hurting so much; it feels as if I am moving up and down, as if I am about to fall over.

'Peggy, I can't move,' I call over to her.

'What is it, dear? Just put one paw in front of the other, you know how to do it,' and she looks at me and sniffs the air.

Slowly, I put my port front and port back leg towards her, then my starboard legs. I feel, if this is what ill feels like, then I must feel ill. I take one step, a bit closer to Peggy. All my legs hurt. Ow. I mewl.

Peggy looks at me again. 'It must be your whiskers, dear heart. All your whiskers have gone.'

I try to twitch them, but can't feel anything. My head feels both heavy with the pictures of the men and the red and the smoke, but it feels light too. Port. Starboard. Port. Starboard. I reach Peggy and nuzzle up next to her, glad of her warmth. Maybe if I just close my eyes and… smoke and flies and, no, I can't do it. I will just sit here, just lie here…

More banging from outside and Peggy and I both jump. George rushes outside. Don't go, George! Some of the other sailors sit up, very quiet and still. Bang! Bang! We wait and wait. I try to put my head right under Peggy's belly, to try to make everything go away.

Footsteps, and George comes rushing back in. 'Those blasted Commies. It isn't safe for the Consort to stop. They've been hit as well. Badly damaged. They've headed back.'

All the sailors in the room sigh. It seems to get darker and smaller. More smell, less air to breathe. Peggy's ears droop right down.

'So does that mean we're stranded here?' I hear someone call out.

'No, it darned doesn't.' Another voice. 'Leave it with me. I'll get a transmitter working. We'll get a signal out.'

'There's always a bottle,' someone else shouts, and the sailors, the poor sailors covered in black and red and those wrapped up in cloth like the snake man, all laugh.

As they stop laughing I look round at their faces. When I first came on board they all seemed so fresh and clean and new. Even I felt new. Now I feel ill and I hurt all over from top to tail. They must too. They don't look new anymore. Or clean. They are dirty, smelly and they all have sad eyes. I realise I am a long way from where I am from, but they all must be too. A long way from Blighty and the king, their brothers, girl-brothers and mothers.

I see the Captain lying on a table asleep; Gurns busy, busy; McCunnell, all quiet and curled up on the floor. I walk slowly over to where he is sitting. Peggy lifts her head off the floor. Port legs, starboard legs, over I walk until I eventually reach McCunnell. I lie down next to him. He looks down, but I don't know if he sees me. Then I feel his hand on my head. Soft… Smoke… Sailors falling… JoJo...

I wake up when I hear footsteps and voices.

'We've sent a message out!' They are either shouting, or my ears still hurt. 'We managed to get a low power set working, but then we discovered all the darned aerials have gone. So Strain and French here hung some wire out of a scuttle and it worked!'[66]

'And?' Gurns asks.

'We got a message that HMS Black Swan and HMS London are on their way up,' French answers.[67] 'And I heard Weston say we've lightened the ship enough now to refloat it and move down river.'

At that moment I hear a rumble coming from underneath my paws. The engines! They're starting up. The ship grumbles and rumbles into life. It creaks and rattles. Peggy trots over to me.

'Hope they've filled those holes in,' she nuzzles me. 'I don't want us to sink after everything that's happened.'

'Maybe we should go outside again and take a look?' I ask her, but she shakes her head straight away. I am glad she does really. I am hurting outside and scared inside. With another loud groan, louder than all the sailors, the ship heaves and I can feel it shake and shudder. We're moving!

'Shan't be long now,' Peggy mutters. Then we hear the sound of loud bangs again. 'Oh, I spoke too soon,' and she lets out a loud noise of her own. All we can do is lie there; the sailors groaning, the ship moving slowly, Peggy and me looking, at each other, at the sailors. This is the first time I have wished I wasn't here.

I hear bang, bang, bang and feel us moving slowly, slowly. All of the sailors who are able are listening to the noise outside until, yes, it's getting quieter. We must be moving away from the bangs. We haven't sunk. We've done it!

'And now the Black Swan and London just have to get to us,' Peggy says. She scratches herself. I wish I could, but I know I am hurting and still too sore. Slowly, she lifts herself up. 'I think I may go and explore now. Now it's, um, safer,' and off she trots, her tail between her legs. I think I know where she is going. McCunnell mutters something,

---

[66] Lieutenant Jock Strain, an Electrical Specialist, led much of the damage control and repairs, rigging up a complete system of 24 volt lighting through the ship. He was promoted to Lieutenant Commander whilst the Amethyst was trapped on the Yangtze.

[67] HMS Black Swan - sister ship of the Amethyst, it was launched in 1939 and scrapped in 1956. It was the lead ship of the Black Swan class of sloops of the Royal Navy. French was the only telegraphist left on board.

but I don't know what he says. Peggy returns carrying something in her mouth. I was right. She looks both happy and sad.

'I found these biscuits.' She tries to make her tail wag. I try to eat some, but my throat is still very dry and sore. I nibble. I cough. The sailors groan. Peggy eats all of her biscuit. And some of mine. We lie there. And wait.

Damage to HMS Amethyst
Photo courtesy of Lieutenant Commander Stewart Hett

Damage to HMS Amethyst
Photo courtesy of Lieutenant Commander Stewart Hett

19/ One hundred and one sleeps

I am surrounded by unhappy. When we heard that the Black Swan and London were only a few miles away, all of the sailors below deck who were able, sat up, smiled and waited. Our ship had been refloated and we had managed to sail a bit further down the river to where it was safer. Peggy was excited at the picture of getting off the ship. I heard some of the injured sailors say they were looking forward to being able to go back to the places where they are from. I was trying to put my paws on the floor and move so it would hurt a bit less and to try and stop myself from feeling all wobbly. George was telling me about his family back home.

But the ships weren't able to rescue us in the end, not like how George had rescued me all that time ago. Gurns said that the Commies, the humans who were attacking us, the ones Chairman was with, had attacked the Black Swan and London as well. They had been hit; some of their sailors had been injured and died, so they both had to sail away, just like the Consort. It made me feel more than bad to see the sailors change from being excited like I am when I play to being so unhappy. They seem as sad as I was when JoJo died.

Died. Dead. Gone. When humans or those you love aren't there anymore. George and Peggy told me that had nearly happened to me. I wonder what it feels like to be dead and gone. Does it feel the same as it does for those who have been left? I think that is why so many of the sailors look so sad on here. Many of their friends are gone, and now we are left here waiting for ships that come to rescue us, only for them to have to turn around again. I wonder if the sailors on here have started to see bad pictures too. Sometimes when I sleep, or try to sleep, in the lower deck where they are, I hear them cry out, or see them suddenly sit up and look around. In the dark I can see their eyes, all big and round and scared. Sometimes they are wet, like George's were.

After the ships did not rescue us, a plane landed on the sea. How strange. I have seen them fly in the sky but not land on water. It looked like a big bird. The plane had a doctor on board.[68] The plane didn't stay long though. As soon as it landed, the bangs all started up again and so it flew off pretty quickly. The doctor must be very brave to jump onto the ship while the Commies were firing.

A few days later a small boat also came with another human who was to be our new Captain. The boat took more injured sailors away even though they didn't want to leave the ship; they all wanted to stay on here and help.

The humans who helped the sailors get off the Amethyst are called Nationalists. They are the ones the Commies were firing at, trying to make them dead. They must have thought we were the same, even though, from what I saw, the Commies look more like the Nationalists than the sailors on here do. Why do humans who look like each other want to hurt each other? Why does anyone want to hurt each other?

George said when we moved the ship some of the Nationalists came over on boats to help, but they were attacked as well. One of them was hurting so much from being hit by one of the big, scary flies, that he even tried to kill himself by swallowing his own tongue. I don't really know why someone would do that, would try to make themselves stop. When George told me, I felt my tongue and tried to move it back, but I couldn't even begin to do it. I thought tongues were for licking and cleaning, not for trying to make yourself stop?

The new Captain is called Kerans.[69] When he arrived on the ship, George carried me under his arm and we went with another sailor called

---

[68] Flight Lieutenant Michael Fearnley RAF - medical officer who was flown from Nanking to the Amethyst by a Sunderland flying boat after Surgeon Lieutenant John M. Alderton was killed on board ship.

[69] Lieutenant Commander John S. Kerans had a distinguished naval service having enlisted in the Royal Navy in 1932. He had China experience which was to prove invaluable in the months to come, having served on the China Station in 1935 on the cruiser HMS Cornwall and again in 1937-39 on the sloop HMS Lowestoft. He was present in Shanghai and other ports during the Sino-Japanese War and served temporarily in the gunboat HMS Ladybird on the Yangtze River in 1937. After the war, he returned to the Far East serving in Security Intelligence at Hong Kong and, in early 1949, he was sent to Nanking as Assistant Naval Attaché. Allegedly he was a dipsomaniac with a volcanic temper and the Navy couldn't really handle him, so they stationed him in a dull job there. Right place, right time when Amethyst urgently needed a new Captain! Kerans later became a Conservative MP for The Hartlepools and served one term.

Hett to say hello to him. George says Hett is an Officer, which means he is more important than most of the other sailors on board. Kerans spoke to George and Hett, but he did not say hello to me. I think he is very strict, even more strict than the other Captain, but George said the sailors need someone to take charge, to make us and the Amethyst shipshape again. I have heard that before. Now I know it means better and ready.

Kerans told some of the sailors to place charges all around the ship, so if anything was to happen to us all then the ship would be blown up. Humans trying to swallow their own tongue, Kerans saying we should do to the ship exactly what the Commies were trying to do. I don't understand any of it. He spoke to all the sailors in the mess and those who were still wrapped in cloth below deck. He gave them all a drink called Horse's Neck.[70] It looked and smelt like the brown drink the first Captain used to have. I don't like the smell of it, but Kerans and some of the other sailors seem to like it. It makes them stop being sad, for a short while anyway. I don't know why it is called Horse's Neck though. I know a horse is a creature so maybe it comes from them? I wonder if there is a drink called Cat's Neck as well.

Another time I saw some of the sailors smile was when Kerans told them someone called a journalist in Hong Kong had heard of what was happening to us. The journalist told the world about it and now the whole world knows where we are, but can't do anything about it. How can one human tell the whole world something anyway? That's a lot of telling. And how could a whole world even help us now?

The only other time the sailors were happy was when they were told of some of our friends who had swum to the land when we first became stranded. They'd had to walk across land that had things in called mines which bang and explode if you stand on them. None of them had

---

[70] Brandy and ginger ale. Only Commissioned Officers actually had a drinks bar. Sailors had a tot of rum issued once a day. Lieutenant Commander Hett arranged a special issue of rum to those with the difficult job of preparing the dead for burial.

exploded though so all the sailors were OK.[71] But the rest of the time, the sailors just look unhappy.

Some who have left the ship and those who are not... dead... are now in a place called a hospital, in Shanghai, the place where we were before it all became scary and bad. The sailors were told that Captain Skinner and some of the others had died too. Died. Dead. Gone. When humans or those you love aren't there anymore. Ginger was one of the sailors who died. That made me very sad when George told Peggy and me. Some of the other injured sailors were taken back to Hong Kong on an American ship called the Repose.[72] That's a ship that comes from the same place as Pauloni. I hope the sailors on that ship were as nice to them as Pauloni is to Peggy and me and that they looked after them.

And now we have been on here for a long, long time. I am starting to feel better though. My back and head are still sore and my paws still hurt when I place them on the floor, but I can move around. I feel different as well. I feel a bit like I did when I met Lilette. I want to scratch and bite again, only this time I know why. I think about Chairman and the Commies and what they did to Ginger, to everyone. I think of what Chairman did to JoJo. I don't know why the Commies wanted to do that to us. Maybe it is because they think the place where they are from would be better if we were not there; maybe that is what Chairman thought too. But they are wrong.

And then I think of the rats. I think of them running around, eating all the sailors' food, not caring about them and making the sailors even more ill. I didn't used to think some creatures were better than others, but now I'm not so sure. If Peggy and me can be friends then why can't other creatures or humans be friends too? But if one creature or human wants to get rid of another one then that means they are bad. It should be the bad ones, not the good ones, who go away, I think. If

---

[71] Telegraphist Robert 'Bob' Ernest Stone, one of 50 crew ordered overboard, later reported that they made their way to safety through perilous, un-manned minefield Rose Island and days of walking across mountainous terrain before being found by Chinese Nationalists. The wounded were escorted to a nearby hospital and the rest to the next town where trucks were waiting to take them to the nearest train station to enable them to travel to Shanghai safely.

[72] A United States Navy Haven class hospital ship. It served as a base hospital ship in Shanghai and Tsingtao, China, supporting the occupation forces in northern China.

creatures or humans do not care, or want to cause hurt, then they need to be stopped. So that is why I need to stop the rats. It would be better for the sailors if the rats weren't on this ship. I have to kill them. I understand that now.

Mao Tse Tung must have told lots and lots of them to come on board. I have even seen them nibbling the toes of the poor sailors down below. That is why Peggy was looking happy and sad when she came back with some biscuits when we did not get rescued. She said she had seen them running around too. 'Like cats who've got the cream.' Those words again. I still don't know what they mean. Maybe it means like rats who've got the biscuits? But it doesn't matter. I know what I need to do.

So, as the sailors and I slowly start to get better, I prowl round the ship. I know I cannot run fast but, whenever I smell that I am near a rat, I hide and I wait. After smelling them, I hear them, snuffling and scratching on the floor. Then I see one. A pink twitching nose. My ears twitch too. I crouch, my claws stretch straight out and then... I spring! Forward, my claws digging into its back, just like the scary monsters in Singapore did to me. But I am doing this because I have to and because it is the right thing to do.

The first time I did it and caught a rat I very nearly felt sorry for it and I was going to let it go. But then I thought of Chairman and his one green eye, I thought of the sailors and how ill they look and I kept on biting and clawing until it stopped moving. I know I could not have done it a long time ago, but I can do it now. I do it to protect my friends and to do my job. Finally, I am a cat who's got the rats.

I walk all around the ship, along the deck and down below. I sniff. I wait. I hunt. Then I clean myself. I sit or lie with the sailors and, when they are asleep at night time, I hunt again. One time Atkins showed one of the rats I had killed to some of the other sailors.

'Brilliant work,' Gurns said. 'Getting rid of the enemy for us. Keep it up.'

Sometimes, when I am not doing my job, I sit with the sailors when they are listening to something called a radio receiver. They all stand around a box and humans speak to them and there are lovely sounds like back home in the place where humans moved around and my bottom wanted to wiggle. I think it is magic. The sailors don't use it very often though because it uses power, but when they do it seems to help make them smile. They listen to voices coming from very far away. George says it helps him and the others to think of home, just like when I lie on them or get stroked it makes them think of those they love back home. I know that too because George told me.

In between hunting and being stroked, we just all wait. And wait. And wait some more. It doesn't hurt as much now when I put my paws on the floor. Peggy says I don't have my eyebrows anymore. Maybe that is why it hurts when I close my eyes? I don't like to close my eyes much anyway, even though George says I need to because it will help me to get better. I don't like to close them because sometimes I see JoJo or Lilette, but sometimes I just see Chairman. I see his green eye glinting and then I see the scary flies and hear the bangs. But then I just hunt the rats even more. George says it helps the sailors when they see dead rats on the ship. It seems strange to me that they would want to see dead things though.

I try to comfort the sailors too by lying next to them. When I see JoJo in my pictures and he does the same to me, I know how it makes me feel, so I want the sailors to feel it too. I know I can't lick them and try to make them clean, but I can lie there and if they want to stroke me on my head then they can. Some of them want to and seem to like it when I go over, but others just want to be left alone.

Just like when I first met McCunnell and I could tell that he did not like me, I think I can tell which sailors want me to be with them and which ones don't. As my whiskers slowly start to grow back, I twitch them and I know which ones to go and lie on, or next to. I still like to sleep on top of George though, so sometimes I sleep on him and other times I stay with the poorly sailors. 'Thanks, Simon,' some of them say. 'What would we do without you? Keeping our spirits up.'

I no longer hear the screaming monsters in my head. Instead I can hear noises and sounds on the ship, just like I used to. Just like my whiskers, I can see that the hairs on the sailors' faces are growing too. They don't look pink and clean anymore. That all seems like a long time ago. They have hair on their heads and round their mouths. Maybe they will turn all furry like me? And then maybe they will start to use their tongues to clean themselves as well? I don't know.[73]

When Kerans came on the Nationalist boat, the sailors hoped he would bring food and water, but all he brought was some paper with lots of squiggles on it. George said we were rationing our food. I remember that word - the first Captain used it. It means not eating very much at all. But now there is not much food for anyone, not even for Peggy and me. Her belly does not wobble as much anymore. The sailors are on half

---

[73] Water was short but sailors were still able to shave. Sailors had to ask permission to grow facial hair.

rations which means they can only have a very small amount of bread every day. Me and Peggy get even less than they do.

I don't think Kerans likes me very much. He is always busy, or shouting; he doesn't seem to want to stroke me or even say hello. Sometimes he gets in a small boat, goes away and then comes back again. George says it is because he is going to see some Commies called Colonel Kang and Major Kung.[74] Whenever Kerans goes I wonder if he will come back or if the Commies will just keep him. Strange how he goes to see the ones who wanted us all dead. He must be very brave. He always comes back though, but when he does he is *very* angry.

I don't quite understand what Kerans talks about, but he says that the Commies will not let us be rescued. The Commies say they attacked us because we attacked them first, but I know that is not true or even real. I was with JoJo. Peggy said we were just sailing down the Yangtze River to help the Consort when all the banging started. If Kerans says to the Commies that we fired first then they will let us go, but Kerans is not going to do that because that did not happen. So, right now, it is more important to be true and real than to pretend, even though we might be able to sail away if Kerans said that. I wonder if I would be true and real if I were him. I don't think I like this adventure anymore. If by pretending it meant I could be with Uboat again, or Lilette, then I think I might just pretend.

It is very hot now on the ship as well. Everywhere I go it is hot, hot, hot. The stowage, the engine room, the stores, the mess, the lower deck. Gurns said it is because the ship does not have much oil. It was oil that was in the water that the sailors jumped into. Even though the oil made some of the sailors go under the water, this ship needs oil to make it move. So oil is both good and bad I suppose.

Whenever I go out on deck there are lots of very tiny flies everywhere. I can see clouds of them above, and on, the ship. And when they land on the sailors' arms or faces, the sailors hit them - smack! Sometimes the flies leave little red patches on the sailors. I hear the flies make a whizzing sound and the sailors try to jump out of their way. I don't like them. Not as much as I don't like the huge scary flies, but these ones still try to land on me and bite me, so I go back inside the ship until they've gone. But then my fur is too hot and, however often I lick myself, I can't cool down. I don't know where to put myself. Peggy doesn't

---

[74] Colonel Kang - the chief Chinese negotiator. Major Kung - the local Communist Commander.

either. I try to make her happy as well as the sailors. Sometimes she nuzzles me, but sometimes she tells me to go away.

George says he and the other sailors are happy to have me around though, which means they like it that I am on this ship. What did the first Captain say to me all that time ago? That we all have a job to do, including me. Well, my job is to hunt the rats so, until we all get rescued, that is what I do now.

****

It is still hot. *Really* hot. Everyone is hungry and has lots more fur, including me. I can walk now; it does not hurt as much anymore and I do not feel as ill. I can even jump up the stairs. I do not know how long we have been on here, not moving. But most of the sailors are now able to walk around more too. Sometimes I go into the ops room and watch French tap, tapping on something. He taps it very fast and it makes a 'clack, clack' sound, a little bit like when Peggy and me walk around the ship. Whenever I am in the ops room and French is talking to Kerans, he tells him he is sending signals out and then says what messages he gets back. Maybe that is what the tap, tapping is for. Kerans always scratches his head and shouts. I don't think he is shouting at French though. He is just shouting because he wants us to be moving.

Peggy, me, George, Gurns and some of the other sailors are in the mess. I can tell by the smell of what they are drinking that it must be Horse's Neck. Even though I don't like the smell of it, and certainly not the taste - George put some on his finger once and I had a lick, but it was horrible - it smells better than the ship smells now. Whilst we have been waiting, waiting, the sailors often roll little papers and set fire to them. It is smoke that comes out, not fog. I know that now. I still don't like it though. Sometimes they shout at each other if one of them has more than another sailor and they don't share the papers fairly. They are sitting around a table and holding things in their hands. I don't know what they are. They all look the same to me. Why are they looking at things that are all the same? Kerans comes in.

'Any news, Captain?' Atkins asks, knocking back some of his drink.

'We're sending messages back home, but there's no movement I'm afraid. Still a darned cat and mouse game those Commies are playing,' Kerans answers, gruffly.

Cat and mouse? So where are the cats and where are the mouses? Maybe he means rats?

'Can't stay here forever though, waiting for them to budge,' Kerans continues. 'Even on rations we don't have much fuel left. Any of that for me?' he asks, pointing at Atkins's drink.

Atkins pours him a glass.

'So what are we going to do?' Gurns puts one of the things he is holding onto the table. He's put it the other way around though. It has nine - or is it ten? - black marks on it. Ah, I see now, they're learning about numbers as well.

'Leave it with me,' Kerans snaps. 'They brought me on here to get you boys out and, by Christ, that's what I intend to do.' He drinks all his drink back in one go. 'I'm currently working on a plan. You'll receive my orders soon enough. The early bird catches the worm and all that,' and he marches out.

Birds? Worms? I like Kerans talking about all these creatures, but I like the sound that he has a plan even more.

George looks at the thing that Gurns has placed on the table.

'Is that your go, Gurns?' he asks.

'Sure is. You got anything to match that?'

George takes a thing from his hand and puts that down too. It has a picture of a lady on, only with a head coming out of her bottom as well. How funny. Maybe they're not learning about numbers after all? Maybe they're learning about monsters?

The sailors all laugh. Perhaps this is a funny monster and not a scary one?

George rubs my head. 'Do you want to play as well, Simon?' he asks. How can I play? All the sailors have five fingers on one hand. I lift up my starboard paw and look at it. I only have - I look down - one, two, three, four.

'Do you remember when you first brought him on board, George?' Gurns chuckles. 'And he put his paws in the jug. I knew then he'd be a welcome member of the crew.'

'Sure do,' George answers. 'All seems a long time ago now.'

Gurns and the others all nod. 'Think you've done a great job though, Simon,' he says. 'Looking after all of us.'

'Horace Walpole used to have a cat,' Gurns tells the others, 'Called Selina. He told a poet called Thomas Gray about her and he wrote a poem.' Gurns gives a little cough. '*Ode to the death of a famous cat, drowned in a tub of goldfishes...* '[75]

Gulp. I don't like the sound of that.

'Do you know why black cats are considered unlucky?' George asks the others as he picks up the numbers and the monsters and rubs them all together. They shake their heads.

'James Joyce wrote a poem. *The Cat and the Devil*. The devil promises to build a bridge for people in return for the first person to cross it to be his slave, but the mayor sends a cat... '[76]

I think George means a human when he says person. I know what a cat is though, of course.

'The cat jumps into the devil's arms,' George continues, 'And becomes friends with the devil, so that's why... ' All the others make an 'Oooh' sound. 'Good job you're not all black then,' George says to me.

No, I'm black and white. So maybe that means some of me is lucky and some of me is unlucky?

'What about Mrs Chippy?' Atkins pipes up.

'Who's that?' George asks.

'Shackleton's cat. She went on the expedition to the Antarctic with him. But when it got too cold and they had to move they had to get rid of everything they didn't need so, bye bye, Mrs Chippy... '[77]

---

[75] Horace Walpole - an English art historian and Whig politician (1717 – 1797). In February 1747, his cat fell into a Chinese porcelain goldfish tub and drowned. Walpole was upset and his friend the poet Thomas Gray (1716 – 1771) wrote an elegy to cheer him up.

[76] Irish novelist and poet (1882 - 1941). He wrote *The Cat and the Devil* in 1936 for his grandson Stephen.

[77] A hardy tomcat from Glasgow - nicknamed Mrs Chippy despite being male. Her owner Henry McNeish, a shipwright and carpenter, was recruited by Sir Ernest Shackleton in 1914 for his third Antarctic expedition on the Endurance. When Endurance was shipwrecked and the crew had to head for land, Shackleton told them that anything that was not of use to the expedition was to be put down. Reports differ as to whether the crew were forced to poison or shoot Mrs Chippy.

'I don't think any of us would have left you out in the cold.' George rubs my head again. It is still a little bit sore, but I don't mind.

I think I would quite like to be in the cold, even though I do not want to be away from George and Peggy and my friends. But I do think I would like to smell a different smell, and to not be so hot. I am just about to head out on deck again when Kerans comes rushing back in.

'Just to let you all know I sent a signal to the C-in-C:[78]

''Grateful your advice on my action if menaced by a typhoon,' and have just received this:

''The golden rule of making an offing and taking plenty of sea room applies particularly.'[79] Just so you all know.'

Know what? What *is* he talking about?

Kerans nods at all the sailors, turns on his heel and strides back out.

---

[78] Admiral Brind was the Commander in Chief of the Far East station at the time of the Yangtze Incident. Kerans was in communication with him to update him on Amethyst's situation and progress.

[79] The actual coded message sent by Kerans, hinting that he was planning an escape. And the response from C-in-C, implying that Kerans could go ahead with this plan.

Simon, Peggy and the crew whilst the ship was trapped – July 1949
Photo courtesy of Lieutenant Commander Stewart Hett

20/ Splash

I am walking around the deck. I asked Peggy if she wanted to walk round with me, but she said she didn't. The hotter it is, the less she wants to move. The less we eat, the less she wants to move. I wish I could make her happier. Even though I am very hungry, I still want to move around, to get away from the heat and the smell coming from the inside of the ship. Now that my legs don't hurt anymore, now that I am the opposite of... being dead... I want to move around as much as I can. I still cannot run very fast - I don't think I will be able to run properly again - but I like the feeling of walking round and round the ship, jumping out of the way of the tiny, whizzing flies.

A boat has arrived and its men are helping us. When it first came I was scared, but George says it's OK as they have come to give us some oil. The huge round things are called barrels and the oil must be in that. Hett, Gurns and some other sailors are lifting and carrying the barrels up, up and then rolling them along the deck of the ship. They must be *very* heavy. After the sailors have rolled a barrel, they stand it up and hold it over something. They stand there for a long time, then they put the barrel down and fetch another one. They have been doing it all day and their bodies are all wet. They don't even stop to put paper in their mouths and set fire to it.

The crew unloading oil barrels
Photos courtesy of Lieutenant Commander Stewart Hett

We have been on here for a long time now. Every time I see the moon I want to remember how many times I have seen it and add it to all the other numbers, but sometimes the moon isn't there and sometimes I just forget. George has been making little marks next to the pictures on his bed. One every day. When he gets to five, he puts a line through the other four so it looks a little bit like a gate. There are lots of them now.

I have done lots of purring and being stroked. I have killed lots of rats, but I know I still have a lot more to kill. I have sat on sailors' laps and slept next to them. They have looked at lots of numbers and monsters, made lots of scribbles on paper and drunk Horse's Neck. There've been lots and lots of days and sleep and not so many biscuits or fun. But at least I have been moving around and getting better and the sailors have been too.

The bridge still looks damaged when I walk round it. I know the ship works though because days and days ago we were able to sail away from the really scary place with the bangs to this part of the river, but I wonder how long the ship will be able to sail for again. It doesn't look like it could get very far when I stand here and see all the broken parts. I trot up to the bridge and see Kerans is in there with Sharpe. They are both talking and scratching their heads. Kerans looks up and sees me.

'Get out, cat!' he shouts in a very loud voice. 'No time for you in here.' I jump and hide under a loose swinging bed that is lying on the deck.

'No need to shout, sir,' I hear Sharpe. 'Look at him hiding now. Trying to get away from you and all your noise. Besides, he's done a lot of good for morale on here.'

'Tsk,' I hear Kerans snap back. 'A hammock to drown out any noise. What a ridiculous idea. Coward.'

After I have stopped shaking I peep out from under the swinging bed and make a dash for the starboard side. I walk quickly right round and reach the stern. There is someone standing there. It looks like they have one leg over the railing and they are wobbling, wobbling. I creep up to them very, very slowly. My back is pressed right back against the ship. There is a bag on the deck and I have to squeeze right past it to get to the stern. I get up as close as I can and I look to see who it is. It's McCunnell! What is he doing? I know that the sailors and their legs should be on the ship, not like that. If Peggy or me did that we would fall right overboard. Why is he doing this?

Quickly, or as quick as I can, I turn and walk fast, walk fast back up to the bridge. I reach it and stand in the doorway. Kerans sees me again. 'Hsss. Go away, cat,' he shouts at me again. 'Can't you see we're busy?' But I am not scared this time. I stand there, give him my best stare and mewl.

'Go! Be off with you.'

Still standing. Still staring. Being brave. I let out another mewl.

'Maybe he wants something?' Sharpe looks at me and then back at Kerans.

'Aye. Maybe he's hungry. Well, we're all darned hungry,' Kerans snaps back.

I mewl again.

Sharpe steps towards me and I turn to head back to the stern. He follows me with Kerans close behind. I walk fast again, jump over... that... and turn my head round to see if they are still following. I mewl again and move even faster. I reach the stern with Sharpe and Kerans not far behind. They spy McCunnell, now with both his feet on the gunwale.

'McCunnell!' Sharpe shouts.

McCunnell turns around and sees us all. His eyes are wet and he doesn't look happy at all. Sharpe rushes forward and grabs him. 'Hey, what're you doing? Come on.'

Sharpe lifts McCunnell and drags him back. They both collapse in a heap on the deck. McCunnell is shaking.

Kerans reaches into his pocket and produces something shiny. 'Perhaps you need a tot of this.' He passes it to McCunnell. McCunnell wipes his eyes with the back of his hand and glugs it all back. He looks at Kerans, Sharpe and me and gives a very tiny smile.

'I'm sorry,' he says.

Kerans bends down and strokes my back. Ow. It is still a bit sore. I wish he had stroked my head instead.

I leave them and wander off to find Peggy. Seeing McCunnell dangling over the stern has given me another picture. I want to tell her about it. I find her in her box in the stowage, all curled up.

'Peggy. Peggy. Wake up.'

She doesn't move.

'Peggy.' I manage to jump right into the box and land on top of her.

'Grrr. Snuffle. Biscuits. What is it?' She wakes up and flicks her ears.

'I think it's time we got rid of the rats. Once and for all.'

'Can't it wait, dear?' She nuzzles me. 'I'm most awfully comfortable in here.'

'No, no. We've got to do it now. The sailors don't have much food and what they have we need to save for them, as much as we can.'

'Oh, all right, all right. If you insist.' She slowly gets up and clambers out of her box.

We pad down to the galley and look around. I can't see any rats, but I can smell them.

'OK, any food you see, any bread, anything. Fetch what you can and we'll make another trail. Then we'll go to the stores and get some more. Biscuits, bennies, anything. We'll have to use a little bit of food in order to save lots of food. We'll make a trail right up to the stern.'

Peggy is sniffing around. It isn't long before she finds some bread. It looks a bit green.

'Will this do?' she asks.

'Yes. Yes. Anything. And please don't eat any this time.' I feel like Kerans. Taking charge. Knowing what needs to be done.

We get the bread and find some more and some more. We break it up with our paws and with our teeth, as small as we can. We carry it all in our mouths and take it up near the stern. The bag is still there. Good. We make a trail of food in the small space between the bag and the side of the ship before going back to the galley and rummaging around for more food. We find some biscuits and some rice.

'Bite the biscuits, Peggy. Make them small. But no eating.'

'OK,' she grumbles. And she bites them and then presses her paw on them to make them even smaller. I collect some of the rice – ugh, it doesn't taste very good - and take that up to the stern too. We have made a trail and a nice pile of food on the stern. As we add to it, the pile gets bigger and the trail gets longer.

'Like Hamsel and Petal,' I smile at Peggy.

She gives me a funny look.

Back to the galley, more rice, as much as we can find. Then into the store room to see what we can find in there. We find some things that don't smell very nice and other things that do. Then we trot back to the stern, dropping and adding the food to the trail.

Peggy is panting, whether from thirst or from being tired, I don't know. My back legs are hurting; this is not as easy it was before, but at last we have done it. Now there is a long trail of some yummy and some not so yummy food and a nice pile on the stern. But it doesn't matter. I know the rats will eat anything, even the toes of the poorly sailors.

'I suppose we have to hide and wait again, like last time?' Peggy asks.

'Yes. And no falling asleep like before either.'

'Oh, don't you worry about that. I feel quite perky now, don't you know?' She nudges me. I wish her belly would swing like it used to. We hide and we wait. We are right near the stern. I look up and out from my hiding place. The sky is still blue, but I think it is getting dark. I can hear the little flies. They always seem to appear when it starts to get dark, just like when some birds used to appear back home as it started to get hot and then they would go away when it got even hotter.

I look at Peggy. She has her eyes open. That's good.

'What are you doing?' I ask her.

'What do you mean, what am I doing?' she answers. 'I'm thinking. I know I said I am a doer and you are a thinker, but I seem to be doing a lot more of that these days.'

'And what are you thinking about?' I ask her again. I wonder what dog pictures are like.

'Oh, you know,' she replies. 'Stuff.' And she lets out a little parp.

'Sshh. Don't do that. You might scare the rats away. Or me.'

'Hmm. I don't think I could scare you away now, Simon. Brave little cat.'

We fall quiet. We wait. Both with our eyes open. My ears are back and listening. Peggy's ears are down. Both our noses are twitching.

And then... A familiar squeaking and the running of tiny paws. Squeak, squeak. Patter, patter. My fur stands on end again. My claws stretch out. I might not have five of them to play monsters and numbers with the sailors, but I have four of them to do this. My nose twitches. I can smell them. Peggy goes to growl, but I make her shush.

I peep out and I can see them. I can see them coming. Rats and rats, following the trail, their pink feet and noses and their long tails. Running rats, eating all the food. *Our* food. I don't know how many there are, but there are lots of them. Some of them are up on the stern now, eating from the pile of biscuits and bread, rice and... other things. At the back I can see a big rat. The biggest of them all. Mao Tse Tung. It's him! He is sniffling and moving quite slowly, but he is coming towards us all the same.

I shrink back a little, but still watch them as they pass. More and more of them are running up to the stern. Mao Tse Tung scampers past me. I wait and I think of numbers in my head. Six, seven, eight, nine and another nine and another one, a lady with a head coming out of her bottom, right that will do. Goooo!

I jump out of my hiding place, spring forward and leap up to the stern. Ow! My back, my back legs, but I don't care. All we have is now. Peggy is right behind me. I get to the stern; the rats are all feasting, eating; some of them don't even see me. I stretch my claws out, jump and... I grab one. I bite its back. It doesn't taste very nice, but I don't care. I keep on biting and clawing it until it stops moving; until finally it is dead.

Peggy is lying next to the bag, blocking the way. The rats can't get past her and they are too scared to try and run next to her and over the bag. They run round and round in circles. I grab another one and bite! Hard. And another and another. I catch another with my claws, bite it and add it to the slowly growing pile of dead ones. One rat, two rats, three rats, four. My claws feel sharp, my eyes feel sharp. I feel... alive! I get a feeling like I had with Lilette to miaooowwww! Jump and run and bite. But this is different too. With Lilette it was good. Good good. This is good bad. I bite another rat and throw it onto the pile. They don't know where to run or what to do. Even Peggy catches one with her paw. I take it from her and do what I need to do.

I spy a familiar shape standing behind Peggy. I realise it is George. He must have heard the sound of rats squeaking and come out to see what is happening. He stands back, hiding in the shadows. I look down and see another rat running past me. Grab. Claw. Bite. Throw. If Chairman and the Commies can attack us for no reason then I can attack these rats for one huge, big, good reason. No more eating our food. No more nibbling on the sailors. I bite the back of another one and drag it over and... down into the water you go. Bat! With my paw. I catch another one and drop it over the side of the ship. I see Mao Tse Tung edging back, back but there is nowhere for him to go.

'Wait. Wait!' he hisses.

'I have waited long enough,' I yawl right back at him. Oh, I like that. I reach forward, grab him, and bite the back of his neck and drag him across the stern. My, he is heavy. I bite and I bite. He is scrabbling under my claws, but I don't let go. I bite and he tries to scratch me. I bite and claw him again. Still he doesn't stop moving. Finally, with one extra hard bite, I feel my sharp teeth sink into his horrible neck. Rat's neck, Horse's Neck, neither of them is nice but I know, I know that... to be a cat you have to act like a cat. This is what I am on this ship for. To face my monsters and fears, not to hide from them. I have him by the back of his neck and don't let go. With one last stretch of his pink feet, he goes limp. And stops moving. I let him go. He lies still in front of me. Stopped. Mao Tse Tung is dead.

I look up and hear George shout, 'Well done, Simon! You're a hero!'

Peggy wuffs her wuffiest wuff. 'You've done it!' she cries. 'Really done it this time. Wuff! Wuff! Wuff!'

I puff my chest out and stare at the lifeless body of Mao Tse Tung, the enemy of this ship. I bite into his neck again and half walk, half drag him off the stern, along the deck and up, up, up to the bridge. My back hurts, but I keep walking, keep dragging. There is a trail of red behind me. I reach the bridge, walk right up to Kerans and drop it at his feet.

He looks at the dead rat, looks at me and breaks out into a huge smile.

'I'll consider that a lucky charm. Well done, sailor.'

21/ Escape

I am in the mess deck feeling very pleased with myself. More pleased than I have been since playing with Lilette. McCunnell is in here too. He gives me a smile and a stroke. George notices and whispers to me, 'Blimey, Simon, what's happened to him? He's changed his tune.'

What tune? What is a tune anyway?

Kerans comes striding in, sees me and gives me a wink before turning all serious and coughing. The sailors all stop drinking the strange drink that comes from a creature, making squiggly lines on paper, or looking at monsters' bottoms.

'There's a storm brewing,' he addresses everyone.

'It's been brewing for a long time,' Atkins replies.

'But that means it's good news for us,' Kerans continues.

'Why, sir?' Gurns pipes up. 'The typhoon that passed us a bit ago cost us in oil.'[80]

Gurns must mean a few nights ago, when I woke up because the ship was heaving up and down. I could hear something howling and at first I thought we were being attacked again, but George told me what it was. He said I couldn't go outside because I would get blown right off the ship. I know I have always wanted to fly in the sky, to really fly, but not like that. When some sailors came in from off the deck they looked as if they had all been swimming in the sea.

---

[80] Typhoon 'Gloria' severely battered the Amethyst just a few days before Kerans ordered the escape.

'I'm aware of that, sailor,' Kerans snaps. 'We only have fifty-five tons of oil left. Another typhoon is just passing the China coast now. So, by my reckoning, the banks of the Yangtze will be flooded. That means the Commie batteries on any low lying ground will be removed and the lookouts at Woosung forts will have their heads down.'

All the sailors are staring at Kerans now.

'The moon sets at eleven this evening, that's optimum conditions for darkness.'

'Darkness for what, sir?' asks Atkins.

'So we can make a run for it this evening.'

Some of the sailors gasp.

'I've signalled to HMS Concord down river and they're going to meet us at Woosung.[81] If... no, *when* we get through. And we *will* get through. We'll make sure that the deaths of Lieutenant Skinner and all the other crew weren't in vain.'

All of the sailors stare at the floor for a moment before Gurns looks up and asks, 'Should the Concord be entering the waters, sir?'

'That's all been taken care of, Gurns. Now, there's plenty of work to be done in the next couple of hours. There are only sixty of us on board instead of one hundred and eighty so it's going to be tough. I know there's one fine sailor on here who's been doing some sterling work and I want you all to step up to the mark just like him.'

George whispers to me. 'He means you, you know. You've raised our spirits no end with everything you've done.'

Me? What have I done apart from letting myself be stroked and... doing my job?

Kerans continues. 'I want canvas screens all around the ship. We'll disguise her as a merchant vessel. That should darned well confuse them. And, when we set off, I've instructed black smoke to be put down to confuse them even more.'

'Aye, sir,' Atkins puts his hand up to his head. 'Anything else?'

'Yes. I want you, you and you to fetch some hammocks and sheets and rub soft soap all over them,' and he points at three sailors.

---

[81] HMS Concord - a C class destroyer, initially ordered as HMS Corso. She was launched in 1945, renamed in 1946 and scrapped in 1962.

'Why do you want us to do that?' Gurns asks. 'We don't have much soap left.'

'Just use everything we have,' Kerans snaps. 'Plenty of time for washing after we've made it through. We'll wrap them round the cable so, when it's time to slip anchor, she'll be a hell of a lot quieter. One of you gave me that idea as a means of drowning out any noise.' Kerans looks at me and gives me another wink before returning his gaze back to the men. 'Right. Any questions?'

'Just the one,' French asks. 'Can we listen to the BBC as we're escaping? I like listening to Family Favourites.'

'You can listen to what the hell you like as long as you keep it down and we make it through,' Kerans answers. 'Right. Get to work everybody. We slip the cable at twenty-two hundred. And in one hundred and forty miles - freedom.'

This all sounds exciting. It sounds as if we might be finally making our escape. Another adventure. I hope it's better than the one I'm in because all this waiting and all this bad has just gone on for too, too long. I pad out and go to find Peggy.

She is, as usual, in her box with her monkey. She isn't sleeping though, just staring.

I put my front paws up onto her box and look down at her. She sees me, but barely lifts her head.

'Hello, Simon. Seen any more rats?'

'No. I think I got rid of a lot of them. If I see any more though I'll just… ' and I stretch my claws out.

'Good. Do you want to get in?' she asks.

'No. I think you should come out and watch. Kerans said we're going to make a run for it.'

Peggy's head lifts right up when she hears that.

'Oh good, because, you know, I really don't want to be here anymore. I can't bear it.'

Slowly, she clambers out and we both head out on deck. It is slightly cooler out here and the ship is lit up by the moon. I can see sailors everywhere, draping whatever they can over the side of the ship. No more flags, just dark, dark sheets.

'What are they doing?' Peggy asks.

'Hiding the ship,' I tell her.

'But I can still see it,' she says, puzzled.

'Just wait. You'll see,' and we settle down to watch the sailors preparing for whatever is about to happen next.

'No falling asleep,' I nuzzle her.

'Fat chance of that,' she answers.

We lie on the deck, we watch and we wait. Kerans keeps striding past us, looking up at the sky and at something round his arm. Finally, he calls out to three sailors. 'Slip anchor.'

My heart jumps. 'This is it,' I say to Peggy.

We stand up and run down to the huge chain. It is all wrapped up in hammocks and sheets. Slowly, it starts to move, but it doesn't make the same noise as it usually does. Whatever Kerans wanted the sailors to do must have worked because he is smiling and nodding on the bridge beside Hett. Then his face drops as he sees a brightly lit ship passing us on the river.

'Is that a merchant vessel?' he cries. 'All right, let's wait for it to pass. We can slip behind it. Might give us some extra cover.'

We watch and wait for the other ship to pass. Just as it gets quite small I hear Kerans shout an order again. 'OK, it's high tide and the moon has set, we need to do it now! If we don't, we'll never make it before dawn.'

Slowly, very, very slowly, our ship starts to move. I look up at some of the sailors who are standing around. Apart from the sound of the engine, it is very quiet. Nobody is speaking. One of the sailors has his hands clasped in front of him. The night sky is black; the ship is black; I am black and white. I hope the Commies don't spot me. I duck down behind Peggy. I am trembling.

Slowly, we are moving away from the land and heading down river. I heard Kerans say if we move and they fire at us all the sailors would have to jump into the water and he would set charges. George shook when Kerans said that. And I didn't like the sound of it myself either. Not at all.

'Come on, come on,' I hear someone mutter quietly.

I can see the merchant ship ahead of us, its lights blinking.

'I don't know how far we have to go, but if the escape is like this it will be easy,' I whisper to Peggy. I am not trembling so much now.

'Yes,' she answers. 'Plain sailing.'

Why is she talking about that now? I have seen a plane sail, but that is a ship. Maybe Peggy is getting confused?

The black smoke from our ship starts to settle around us. Just as I start to breathe properly I hear a bang come from the land on the port side. Oh no! I see the faces of the sailors fall.

Peggy whimpers and I hear and smell what she does next.

'What shall we do? Where shall we go?' she cowers. Suddenly, it gets darker. The merchant ship in front of us has put all its lights out. Bang! Bang! It is all dark, but I cannot really see very far because of the smoke. It reminds me of before. Bang! Bang! I am scared now. *Really* scared. And so are the sailors around me. We're not going to make it.

I feel the ship move faster before I hear someone shout, 'The ship! It's been hit!' But they don't mean us. They mean the one in front that we are sailing closer to. There is fire coming from it. They've hit the wrong ship!

Another bang. I can hear something whizz past right in front of the bow and splash into the water. Quick! Quick! Come on! We get closer to the other ship. There are even more flames coming from it now. I feel sorry for the humans on there, but glad that it is not us. Good and bad.

Bang! And our ship judders. I think the bow has been hit. Come on! We sail right past the merchant ship on fire. The land is on the other side of it. If the Commies fire again they will just hit that one and not us. Keep going!

We pass right by it and sail on down the river. The banging stops.

'Quick,' I say to Peggy. 'Let's get below deck while we can.' We both move as fast as we are able, running through the black smoke. I am not scared of this black smoke. I know it is there to protect us, but I am scared of what we cannot see, scared of the Commies who might be able to see us.

Down in the mess deck a few sailors are huddled together. It is very hot and smelly. I can hear a sound. It must be coming through the magic receiver, but I am too scared to wiggle my bottom. The sailors look frightened too. They are wide eyed or pacing up and down with smoke coming from their mouths. I see George and pad over to him. He is shaking, even more than when Kerans said we might have to blow the ship up.

None of the sailors is talking. I think they are just trying to listen to what is going on outside. We can't hear any banging, but they are still quiet, still looking scared. Gurns has his fingers in his mouth and he is biting them. On and on we go. I know we are sailing through the darkness, sailing into the night, but what are we sailing towards?

A noise. But it isn't banging. It is Kerans's voice, coming from somewhere. 'Thirty up.'

I hear some of the sailors sigh. Thirty up what? George strokes my head extra hard. Ouch!

The sailors are all very still. I close my eyes and try to let the sound coming from the radio receiver fill my head. I try to make the pictures in my head change to blue skies instead of darkness. I can feel the ship moving forward, forward. We wait and listen and wait. Kerans's voice again. 'Fifty up. Careful now. We're just reaching Klangyin. It's going to be difficult making our way through the boom. Expect a welcome.'

I open my eyes; the sailors are all looking around; at each other, at the floor. Smoke is coming from some of them. McCunnell is pulling his fingers. Then...

Bang! Bang! Bang!

All the men seem to go very small. McCunnell's fingers are in his mouth. George picks me up and holds me very tight. I don't know who is shaking more, me or him.

Still the noises come. It sounds like it's from both sides now. Bang! Bang! Please don't let us be hit. No more. Please.

Peggy starts to whimper and moves closer to Atkins. He rubs her head and gives her half a biscuit, but she doesn't even want it. 'You're getting too old for this, aren't you old girl?' he comforts her.

Bang!

There is a huge clang from outside. They must have hit us! We're not going to make it.

But we do not stop. We keep moving. Another bang, but no clanging sound. Then, the banging gets quieter. We must have got through. All the men breathe out.

No one speaks until we hear Kerans's voice again. 'Sixty up.'

'Nearly halfway there,' French mutters. 'Just over halfway to go.'

Still we move forward. On and on. The sailors are biting their bottom lips or just sitting there staring. This feels as long as when we were stranded. I wiggle and George sets me down. I walk over to Peggy. We nuzzle each other before I slowly walk in between the sailors' legs, letting them stroke me if they want to.

'Seventy up.'

That's a big number. More waiting, but there are no more bangs. I want to go outside, to see if it's safe. Should I do it? If I count and count in my head and there are no bangs then, yes, I will do it. I will be brave. I think of all the numbers I know, small ones and then big ones. I don't get to seventy but I get to twenteen. I tell Peggy. 'I'm going to go out on deck.'

'Don't do it, Simon. Are you mad? Don't go.'

But I trot out and up the stairs. I step out on deck. It is dark, it is smoky, but there are no bangs. I am scared. I want to be brave. I think of Chairman. I think of JoJo. I run as fast as I can up the starboard side and up to the bridge. Kerans is there with Hett and Sharpe. Hett peers at some papers then looks at the land before peering at the papers some more. George said it is Hett who will decide which part of the river we sail in. I really hope he knows what he is doing. Just as I get on the bridge, I hear the bangs again, coming from both sides of the ship.

'Increase speed,' Kerans shouts.

Faster! Faster! Bangs coming from the starboard, bangs coming from the port. We are sailing through a very narrow stretch of the river. That must mean we are even closer to the Commies. Bang! Bang! Come on! I really don't like this. Even more bangs. Another whizz in front of the bow. But they don't hit us. We push forward. I look at Kerans. He looks angry. I look at Sharpe. He looks scared.

'Eighty up.'

'We're doing well,' Hett calls over to Kerans.

'Not there yet though, are we?' he answers. 'How're we doing for fuel? Where's my Horse's Neck?'

'Just shy of thirty tons,' Sharpe tells him. 'It's over there. Not much left.'

'No. Not much left of either. Increase her speed if you can.'

I wish I wasn't here. I wish JoJo was here. My pictures lurch as much as the ship seems to. We keep going. Sometimes I think I hear bangs when there aren't any. Sometimes I hear bangs when there are. Each time I think of magic, of JoJo, of Uboat or Lilette. I don't think of shadows or monsters.

More black, more smoke. More trembling inside me. At some point, Hett's face changes. 'It's zero two thirty, sir. We've reached one hundred up.'

Kerans puts his mouth over something and repeats what Hett has just said to him. I'm sure I can hear the sailors shouting. Is this good or bad? We have not been hit, so I think it is good. One hundred up must be good. I breathe out again.

Still we sail. On and on and on. I look up and I see the dark of night is being chased away by the bright of day.

'Only Woosung to clear now.' Kerans's voice. 'Keep your eyes peeled for any search lights.'

Through the smoke, the not quite dark, the not quite light, I see... I don't know what they are. Huge, bright lights moving up and down on the dark water, like lots of suns peeping out from behind clouds.

'They're looking for us. Hard a-port. Easy now.'

The lights sweep past us. What will happen if they reach the ship? I watch the lights on the water. They are moving fast, but they don't touch the ship. We move through them. Still they don't touch us. There are no bangs, but it is all still very, very scary.

And then. And then...

'Look ahead!' Kerans shouts. 'I think I see the Concord. By Christ, I think we've made it!'

My ears prick. My whiskers quiver. Does that mean there won't be any more bangs? Have we done it? Have we escaped?

Kerans calls out again. 'Darned good job too. We've only got nine tons of fuel left.'

I stare up at Kerans and Hett. They shake hands, they are both happy. I am surrounded by happy. Kerans has a big, big smile on his face. He looks happier than I've ever seen him before. The Concord flashes at us and Kerans and Hett both break out into laughter. 'Fancy meeting you here.'[82]

Kerans puts his mouth over the thing again. 'Concord in sight and signal has been received. Please send a signal in return: 'Never, never, has a ship been more welcome.''[83]

I run as fast as I can out of the bridge, down the starboard, no - port - oh, it doesn't matter – side and head back to the mess deck. I am moving so fast I can feel my back hurting again, but I don't care because I'm not dead. I even spy a rat on my way back and pounce on it. Bite! Take that. When I reach the mess deck, all the sailors are jumping up and down or moving around, holding each other, just like the men with the shiny buttons and the women who smell nice back in the place where I am

---

[82] Actual message sent by Concord to Amethyst when the Amethyst passes the Woosung forts and is free.

[83] Actual message signalled back in return.

174

from. The sailors are all cheering, so loud it makes my ears hurt. Some of them even have wet eyes although I don't know why because this is all happy, not sad. Peggy is running around in a circle, trying to catch her wagging tail.

I hear French shout, 'I knew we'd made it. The BBC were playing 'Cruising Down The River' on the receiver just as the signal came through.'[84]

George picks me up and spins me round. I am flying, flying, spinning, spinning. 'Oh, you little beauty.' He even kisses me on the nose.

Peggy, me and some of the others go out on deck. We see the Concord and the sailors on it waving at us. I wish I could wave back, but then George lifts up my port paw and does it for me.

Kerans comes down from the bridge to join us and is met with cries of, 'Well done, sir!'

'And well done to you all,' he replies. 'And you too,' and he rubs my head, but doesn't kiss me on my nose. 'I've signalled the C-in-C with the following message: 'Have rejoined the fleet south of Woosung. No damage or casualties. God save the King.''[85]

'God save the King!' the sailors all call back. 'And God save you,' says George to me, quietly.

Later that day, that big, big, best day, Kerans told us all that we had even received a message from King George the Sixth. I remember that silly man Henri telling me about him. The message was: 'Please convey to the Commanding Officer and the ship's company of HMS Amethyst my hearty congratulations on their daring exploit to rejoin the fleet. The courage, skill and determination shown by all on board have my highest commendation. Splice the mainbrace.'[86]

---

[84] Telegraphist Jack French is reported as recalling the song being played. The song was written by two female shop workers, Eily Beadell & Nell Tollerton, in 1945 and was the winning entry in a competition. The song was the No 1 hit in 1949 for Blue Barron (1913 – 2005).

[85] Actual message Kerans sent to the Commander in Chief in Hong Kong.

[86] Actual message sent by King George the Sixth to the Amethyst.

It all sounded too big and confusing for me. But I know what kings are and I know they are important.

'Fancy getting a message from the head of the monarchy,' I heard George say.

I know that head can mean toilet, but it can also mean someone really important - like a king. So if we have received a special message from the head of the monkeys then he must be really, *really* important.

Crew: The four in the middle of the front row are, left to right:
Hett, Kerans, Strain, Fearnley
Photo courtesy of Lieutenant Commander Stewart Hett

22/ Hot and visible

It is Wednesday, the 3rd of August 1949. We became stranded on the River Yangtze on the 20th April and escaped on the 30th July. Even though I don't know what any of this means I know it must be important because George is making squiggles on paper and talking to me. It must be something to do with having lots of biscuits and bread many moons ago, to having hardly any until we escaped.

Many moons ago - I like that. Many moons ago, I was so scared. Many moons ago, there were sailors on this ship who aren't here anymore, like Weston who was injured, and those who aren't anywhere anymore, like Ginger and Captain Skinner. Weston left when Kerans came to take charge. I don't know where Ginger and the Captain have gone to. I just know they are gone, of course. Dead and gone. How sad.

Many moons ago, there were even other humans on here - like that silly man, Henri, with the thing round his neck. Many moons ago, I was chased by scary monsters in Singapore, and before that I met Peggy and, just before that, George found me and brought me on here, just after JoJo...

But there is no moon now. It is day and it is lovely and bright and sunny. Hot, but not as hot as it has been spending moons and moons on the ship. It is hot here, like I remember. We are sailing into Hong Kong, the place where I... used to be from. There are three ships sailing in front of us, but they are all our friends. When I first saw them they had flags on them and I knew they were the same flags as the ones on here. The ship right at the front is called Jamaica, behind that is Cossack, and behind that and right in front of us is Belfast.[87] There are some new sailors on our

---

[87] HMS Jamaica – a colony class cruiser, launched in 1940 and scrapped in 1960. HMS Cossack - a C class destroyer, launched in 1944 and scrapped in 1961. HMS Belfast - the

ship too who came on to help. I don't know why they have come on board, but George said it is good they are here, so both it and they must be.

As we approach the harbour, I hear lots and lots of bangs. I shrink right back when I hear them, but George says they are called Chinese firecrackers and that I shouldn't be scared. I still am a little bit though. Our ship moves faster, or maybe the others move slower, because we sail past them and get right to the front. The place where I used to be from is getting bigger and bigger. When we dock there are many, many humans standing on it, looking up at us. They all have different coloured skin, some like the sailors on here, some like those who wanted us dead but, when they see us, all of them cheer and wave. It is funny to see all the humans cheering and waving, all standing together.

Funny how these are all happy to see us, but there are other humans who wanted to make us all dead. Even though I know what Chairman did to JoJo I still would not want to see him dead. I would just want Chairman to not be so bad.

Lots of them have things round their necks like the silly Henri man. When they hold them up to their faces, even more flashes of sunshine come out of them than from Henri's. Not this again.

'See that,' George points down to them from where we are standing at the bow, with me tucked under his arms. 'That's for you.'

Why, what have I done? Maybe they've heard about the rats?

Bang! Whizz! Crack! The sound of the firecrackers, the flashes of sunshine, the humans shouting, the sailors are lined up waiting for the tongue. Kerans is in front of us, in the same place that the other Captain used to stand.

'As of now, you're all on leave. Twenty-four hours,' Kerans tells them all. The sailors cheer, as loud as the humans down on the dock. Some of them throw their hats in the air.

'The C-in-C has arranged a party for us all. Free gin,' Kerans tells them.

Another cheer.

'And I don't need to tell you all to eat, drink and be merry.'

Royal Navy's last surviving cruiser, launched in 1938 and decommissioned in 1963. She took part in Operation Overlord, supporting the Normandy landings. She is currently moored on the River Thames and operated by the Imperial War Museum.

'What about Bugis Street?' Atkins calls out. Again.

'Go wherever the hell you like as far as I'm concerned. So long as she's not a Commie.'

Laughter and smiles. They walk, no, they *run* down the tongue. Gurns and Hett, French and McCunnell. The humans in the dock shake the hands of the sailors or hug them when they step off the ship. Do they all know each other? As George and me reach the bottom, they hold their things up and go click, click, click right in my face. It blinds me and I don't like it. I close my eyes, but I can still see the sunshine flashes.

'What do you think, Simon?' George asks me. 'Do you want to go to a party?'

I don't know what one is, but I like the sound of it and I want to get away from the sunshine and all the noise. Maybe Peggy should come too? Where is she? Oh there she is, right at the front, her monkey in her mouth, wagging her tail, excited to get off.

I am so pleased to know I am back in Hong Kong that my next few tomorrows and todays get all muddled up amongst lots of sleeps, lots of running up and down the tongue, and lots of cheering from the humans wherever I go with the sailors.

Before I know it, I am heading down the tongue again with George, Kerans and some of the others, Peggy trotting alongside them. Kerans is shaking someone's hand and they are talking and looking all serious. The man he is talking to has white hair and is dressed in a black suit with all shiny buttons on his port side.[88] George goes up to the man who puts his hand out.

'Able Seaman George, sir,' George says to the shiny man, shaking his hand.

'It was Admiral Brind who approved our escape,' Kerans tells George. 'But then he had to make sure that no publicity was given to the fact that HMS Concord came to meet us.'

---

[88] Admiral Brind.

'To prevent a further diplomatic incident, you see,' Brind says, beaming a broad smile. 'Some things are best kept under wraps until they've taken effect.'[89] Then he looks down at me.

'Ah, this must be Simon,' he says to George and me. 'A most excellent morale booster you are.'

I am not a moral buster. I am a cat. Maybe he hasn't seen one of me before?

George and me follow him and Kerans through the cheering crowds. It feels strange to be amongst so many humans again after many moons of being out on the sea, on the seemingly empty ship and stranded on the river. Even more strange to look round at places where I used to play and run around. Would I want to run around here now? I don't know. I don't even know how much I *can* run around now anyway. My paws aren't sore anymore, but my back still hurts a little.

We walk up some stairs into a building that looks like the hotel Peggy liked in Singapore.[90] She is walking alongside Atkins and she seems to like the look of this place too. It smells fresh and clean. Everything is big. Huge lights are hanging down from the ceiling. Pictures of men and ladies are on the walls. And pictures of George and a cat that looks like me as we go past them. Why do they have pictures of me and George in here? And why do they move wherever we move?

I hear a noise getting louder and louder, humans talking over another sound. It reminds me of the wobbly bottom place, or maybe they are listening to the magic receiver. We go through a doorway where the noise is coming from. Humans hit their hands together when they see Kerans, George, me and the other sailors. There are lots of chairs and tables around with the most yummiest looking food on them. I wonder if they have any Whiskers, though I hope they don't have any Horse's Neck.

---

[89] Sir Ralph Stevenson, British Ambassador in Nanking, sent a telegram to the British Foreign Office in Singapore stating, 'No repeat no publicity should be given to the fact that H.M.Ship Concord entered Chinese territorial waters.' The Admiralty press release on 2nd August stated, 'HMS Concord was waiting at the mouth of the Yangtze ready to proceed up river should HMS Amethyst be attacked.' It was only on 12th July 2013 that Mark Francois, Armed Forces Minister, finally confirmed that Concord had sailed 57 nautical miles up river.

[90] The China Fleet Club in Hong Kong.

We sit round a table. I am on George's knee. Some white cloth hangs down from the table and brushes against my nose. It smells very clean, but it makes me want to sneeze. I hear the tinkling of glasses. George's hand is on my head, stroking it. He taps it and whispers, 'Hey, Simon. Something for you.'

I lift my head up and sniff, then I half stand and balance my front paws on the edge of the table. My claws catch on the white cloth and I tug, tug to try and release myself, but I pull the white cloth down instead. Something on the table falls over. Everybody sitting around the table laughs. Was that funny? I've been shouted at for a lot less. I see Kerans sitting across the table talking to the man who doesn't know what I am and pointing at me. Maybe Kerans is telling him what I am?

George passes me a plate with fish on and other things. I sniff round the plate, eating what I like, leaving what I don't. Peggy is underneath the table. I can hear her. Not making her usual noise though, she is just gobbling down lots and lots of food. Just a few moons ago we were stranded on a river with hardly anything to eat and now here we are in a huge, lovely clean place with too much food. Too much food for me, but not for Peggy, of course.

The humans all seem to know which silver shiny things to use and when to use them. I wonder whether I would prefer to play monsters' bottoms and use the shiny things to eat my food or if I am happy as I am. I look at my claws and think about what I have been doing with them. I lick the plate with my tongue. I feel my whiskers brush against the white cloth and my tail hanging down. Then I look at the humans talking to each other and I look at George. He is speaking to someone next to him but, every so often, he stops speaking and he just stares and stares at the white cloth. Then I gaze up at some other humans. They aren't sitting at tables; they are standing up, holding each other, moving around to the wiggly bottom sound that must be coming from the magic receiver somewhere.

I am happy I am me, but there is a bit of me that wants to fly like a bird and, when I look at those humans over there, I realise there is a bit of me that would quite like to be a human too, just for a short while, so I could do what they're doing now.

George taps me on the head again. 'Look what I can see,' and he points to a jug of water. He reaches over, grabs it and moves it closer to us both. I jump up onto the table - should I be doing this? - and stand next to the jug. Everyone sitting around the table stops talking and turns to look at me. I hope I'm not going to get into trouble.

Slowly, I walk around it and sniff the top of it before I stop, crouch back, lift up and rest my two front paws on the jug. I look down inside it. I can't see anything, but I know that not everything that is there can be seen. I put one of my paws in. Ow, ow, it is cold. I feel something. It chinks as it hits the side of the jug. I reach in a bit further with my paw, feel the cold thing that isn't there and use my paw to slide it up the inside of the jug. The cold thing plops onto the white cloth with a little thud and the man with the shiny buttons reaches over and rubs my head.

'Bravo, sir. I can see why you were such good company.'

I do it again. And then again. Each time, the humans smile or hit their hands together. It really isn't so difficult. I don't understand why they can't do it. Maybe they don't like the things in there, so who is it who puts them in then?

Just as I am about to do it one more time, a human walks through the doorway. 'A guard of honour,' George whispers. A what? Kerans taps the jug with one of the silver things and everybody falls quiet. He stands up.

'Ladies and Gentlemen. And sailors.'

Everybody laughs.

'As I'm sure you all know, the crew of the Amethyst and I have endured the most horrific one hundred or so days caught in the crossfire of these ongoing darned shenanigans. Many dear friends and loved ones have been lost, not only from the Amethyst, but from our sister ships too. If it wasn't for the strength, courage and bravery of our men, well, I don't think we would have made it.'

There's lots of nodding and muttering from everyone. I wonder what a sister is.

'However,' Kerans continues. 'It's also thanks to two very special companions on board our ship that we all got through. Simon here... ' I look up, '...has been instrumental in keeping the spirits of our men up and the population of our rats down whilst on board. And Peggy—'

I hear a knock under the table. She must have bumped her head.

'Where is Peggy?' Kerans looks around. Slowly, she comes out from under the table, looking guilty. 'Peggy here has also been a most grateful addition to the crew. If it wasn't for these two, well, I don't know what it would have been like. Earlier, I requested a commendation from the Allied Forces Mascot Club and I have just received a message that it has been approved.[91] Able Seacat Simon here... '

---

[91] The body of the People's Dispensary for Sick Animals that awarded medals to animals displaying acts of gallantry and serving in times of conflict.

That's me.

'...has been awarded the PDSA Dickin Medal, the Animals VC award for gallantry, if you will.[92] I don't have the medal yet of course but, in honour of Simon and everything he has done, and not forgetting Peggy of course, I want you all to stand now and raise a toast to these two fine examples of sailors, while I pin a ribbon on them both and read out a citation.'

As one, everybody in the room stands, looks at me and hits and hits their hands together. Over and over again. Kerans leans forward and tries to attack me with the ribbon in his hand. Uh oh, I must really be in trouble now. He mustn't have liked me putting my paw in the jug of water after all. He was just pretending. Quickly, I jump off the table and hide under it so I don't get attacked. Peggy joins me.

'Fancy meeting you here,' she snorts and resumes eating. From under the table I can hear Kerans shouting at me. 'Able Seaman Simon, for distinguished and meritorious service on HMS Amethyst, you are hereby awarded the Distinguished Amethyst Campaign Ribbon.'

George sticks his head under the table, reaches down, grabs me and plonks me back on the table.

'Be it known that on April 26, 1949,' Kerans is still shouting, but he is smiling at me too. Strange.

'Though recovering from wounds, when HMS Amethyst was standing by off Rose Bay you did single-handedly and unarmed stalk down and destroy 'Mao Tse Tung', a rat guilty of raiding food supplies which were critically short.'

I let out a loud mewl. Peggy comes out to see what all the fuss is about.

'Be it further known that from April 22 to August 4 you did rid HMS Amethyst of pestilence and vermin, with unrelenting faithfulness,' and with that Kerans hands a ribbon to George which he swiftly wraps

---

[92] Maria Dickin, the founder of the People's Dispensary for Sick Animals, instituted the medal to honour acts of animal bravery in wartime. The medal ribbon is green, dark brown and pale blue representing water, earth and air to symbolize the navy, army, civil defence and air forces. The medal is cast in bronze, bears the initials PDSA and 'For Gallantry' and 'We Also Serve'. As of May 2014, the total number of Dickins Medals awarded to animals is 65 - 3 to horses, 32 to homing pigeons and 29 to dogs. Simon is the only cat ever to have been awarded the PDSA Dickin Medal.

round my neck before bending down to wrap one around Peggy's neck too.[93]

I don't like it. It itches. I try to bite it off. Peggy looks up at me, her tail wagging. 'Well? What do you think?' she asks. 'Do I look dashing?'

She looks like Peggy with a ribbon. I ask her what is going on.

'You've been awarded a medal, Simon. For being so brave.'

Am I brave now? Am I really? Finally. But I don't really want a medal. I don't even know what one is. I just want to be with my friends.

I don't know how long we stay in the nice place, but when I leave with George, Peggy and Atkins holding Peggy's toy monkey, it is getting darker and cooler. As we walk along, with Peggy in front, little lights appear from here, over there and up there and start to twinkle and shine. George and Atkins are muttering to each other about something, so I peer over George's arm and mewl down to Peggy.

Her ears prick up and she looks around and up at me. 'Nice to be on dry land again,' she smiles. 'And that food. Oh, delightful.' We turn a corner and she trots off ahead. Through the narrow alleys and streets, we wander in and out of shops. George buys a yellow curved thing and Atkins buys a hairy, round, brown thing. It is nice to be back in a place again where I remember a lot of the smells. It smells of… home. We turn down another alleyway. Peggy is in front until we reach a narrow street that I half recognise.

A shop - ah yes - I know where we are now and Peggy trots right in and sits down on the floor. The owner looks at Atkins and at me in George's arms, then she spies Peggy and she smiles. 'Oh, back again! My, what happen you? You all thin. You need good feed.'

Peggy's tail goes thump, thump, thump on the floor. Atkins and George look around the shop. They keep holding things up and laughing. 'Here. Look at this. It's just like being back home.' Do they both live in a shop where they come from? After George and Atkins give the owner some paper and she gives them a bag we are all ready to leave the shop. Except Peggy, who does not move. George is about to step outside, but I wiggle and wiggle until he looks down at me and then at Peggy. He sets me down and I run over to her.

---

[93] Actual citation that Kerans used to nominate Simon for the PDSA Dickin Award. (Artistic licence was taken re how long it took Simon to pluck up the courage to start killing rats - he was braver than he says!)

'Peggy! Come on!'

She looks at me but she does not move.

'Come on Peggy, we have to go.' I look back over at George and Atkins. They are standing outside, waiting for us. Peggy looks at the floor.

'I'm sorry, Simon, I'm not coming back with you.'

'What do you mean?' I mewl. 'Not coming back? We belong on the ship. We live there.'

'I'm awfully sorry, Simon. Truly I am. I've been doing an awful lot of thinking and not much doing recently. I must have caught that from you.'

But I haven't thrown anything to her. What is she talking about?

'You see, I'm an old dame now, Simon. And after all we've been through, well, I think it's time I moved on to pastures new. It was so beastly to see what happened to all our friends. And what with my Captain leaving and the other Captain dead and now we have Kerans, well, I just don't see why I'm even on there anymore.' She shuffles a little. She looks very sad.

'But we live on there!' I cry.

'No, Simon. *You* live on there. You have a job to do. All I do now is get in everybody's way and wait under the tables for them to drop their food. I don't really do anything. Not anymore.'

'But you're my friend.' I bat her nose with my paw, but she just lies down. 'You're my best friend. You make me happy.'

'No, Simon, you make you happy. I'm just a silly old fuss bag.'

This can't be happening. This can't be right. Not Peggy. Peggy who first looked after me when George brought me on board. Peggy who showed me around the ship and introduced me to Pauloni. Peggy with her licks and her smells and her monkey. Her monkey! Where is it? I run outside the shop to Atkins, look up at him and mewl.

'Hey, hey, what is it?' Atkins looks down. 'Where's Peggy?'

We all go back into the shop.

'Here, Peggy,' Atkins calls to her. 'Here girl, come on.'

But she doesn't move. She just lies there. I look at Atkins and then at her monkey. Atkins must notice what he is holding because he crouches down and places it at her feet. She sniffs it, looks up at George and Atkins, then back at me.

'I'm going to stay here, Simon,' she says quietly. 'The owner has already gone to get me a nice bowl of something scrumptious.'

'No, Peggy! You can't! You can't!' I cry again. But I can tell by the look in her eyes that she won't budge. She won't be coming back with us. George and Atkins call her and call her, but she won't stand up and come over. The owner walks over from the back of the shop and places a red bowl full of food right in front of Peggy. She nudges her monkey out of the way and tucks right in.

'Stubborn as a mule, that one,' Atkins says to George.

She is not a mule. She is a dog. A fat, silly, smelly, lovely, funny dog. My dog.

'Looks like you've got a lodger,' George says to the owner, laughing.

'She been coming here for long time,' the owner replies. 'I always say she welcome to stay.'

'Maybe she is getting a little too old for the ship now,' Atkins says thoughtfully as he watches Peggy tucking in. He turns to the owner. 'Well, if you're sure…?'

George looks down at Peggy too. 'And it seems like she's already made her mind up.'

The owner smiles at George and Atkins. 'She be happy here with me. I look after her good.'

George and Atkins glance at each other, then both slowly bend down to give Peggy a farewell ruffle. I see that there's wet in George's eyes again.

'Come on,' he says quietly, 'Let's go.' They walk out of the shop, but I run right over to Peggy.

'You're really going to stay here, then?' I ask her.

'Mmm, hurr,' she munches. And then looks up. 'It's for the best Simon, really it is. You are all going to be sailing home and I honestly don't think I'll even be able to make it. I think here will be simply a splendid place to spend my golden years.'

I am sad, sad, sad. This is not right. I try one last try. 'But now is all we have.' I mewl again.

'Yes,' she answers slowly. 'And I don't have many 'nows' left. So, everything we had up to now is what we have too. Don't forget that.'

She puts her face up to mine and rubs my nose with hers.

'Bye, Simon, it has been the most awfully good fun spending time with you but, you know what they say, all good things must come to an end.' She gives me a lick.

Why must they?

I give her a nuzzle. One last nuzzle.

'Here's looking at you, kid,' she smiles. A bit of food stuck to her mouth.

I turn and walk out of the shop to join George and Atkins.

'Simon,' I hear Peggy call. I turn around in the doorway and look back at her.

'Remember - you're magic.'

George picks me up. He must know I am feeling very sad because he squeezes me extra tight. Slowly we walk back to the ship. We get lost, we get not lost, we find ourselves near where I used to play. Before Peggy, before everything. First JoJo and now her. Both gone, in different ways, but no less sad. What am I going to do without Peggy? Maybe I could have stayed there with her? But I feel like I belong more on the ship now than I do here, where I am from. Was from. Now I need to carry on being brave, but in a different way.

George rubs my head. I look around at what I used to know and, when we reach the ship, at what I know now. We walk up the tongue. It makes me think of Peggy and her licky tongue. Up and up we go, back onto the deck, back to the place where I am now from. I turn around to have one last look at the port. The port where I used to run and play, before all this. As I look, I am sure I can see, running in and out between some baskets, a beautiful white cat, only much, much fatter than before.

23/ Up to standard

It is grey and cold and I don't know how I feel. We are sailing into Plymouth in England. England is also called home to the sailors on here. The place where they are from. I know it isn't my home, but I suppose it will be now. George said we won't be sailing again on the Amethyst. I am glad about that. It has not been the same since we left Peggy behind. Not at all. She is in the place where I am from and I am going to be in the place where George is from. How strange. I have missed her and missed her all the way from there to here.

We stopped at many places on the way. George said it has taken us nearly the same amount of time to get to England as the time we spent stranded on the ship. I don't know which felt longer, not moving or sailing. When we first left Hong Kong we sailed to Singapore. I didn't get off, of course, not after last time, but it was nice to stand on the bow and look down at all the humans waving. Some of the sailors went to a cocktail party for Horse's Neck and lots of other drinks. Then we sailed to a place called Penang and then Colombo and Aden. After that we sailed through something called the Suez Canal which George said was important, but I don't know why. When we sailed down it, it looked like a very narrow street of water, like the storm drains back in Singapore. We sailed along it for a long, long time before it turned into the big, open sea again. George told me it wasn't real, that it was built by humans, but it looked very real to me.

We stopped at a place called Malta and then a place called Gibraltar. The more we sailed the less hot it became. Sometimes I got off the ship and had a quick look round with George, but mostly I just stayed on board, washing myself and pretending I had not seen all the strange humans who wanted to say hello to me and make me blind with their sunshiny click, clicks. It didn't really matter where I put myself though, because all I did was think about Peggy. And Uboat and Lilette and JoJo of course. I only wanted to be with my dog, my cats and my friends.

When we docked in Gibraltar one of the sailors brought a creature called Hugo on board. He was a rabbit. I had never seen one before. He was quite nice and cute-looking with his big floppy ears and little white blob of a tail. His tail was funny, not like mine at all, but he was very shy and so we didn't speak much. I don't know what happened to him. He seemed to disappear around the same time as the sailors were served up a pie in the mess. They all tucked in, gave me some to try and it tasted delicious.

No matter where we docked though, we were greeted by cheering crowds and happy and smiling faces. It is still good to know that not all humans want to see other humans dead and gone. And everywhere we went I was still surrounded by the flashes of sunshine, by humans coming on board and talking to the sailors and then even more flashes of sunshine. I didn't like it; I don't know why anyone would like it. But everyone seems to want to see me and people everywhere keep saying I am a hero, so I suppose they must like me, even if I don't like their click, clicks.

And now it is cold and we are going to be stopping. For the last time. Well, not stopping. Just not on the ship anymore. We have been sailing for ten thousand miles, George says. That is the biggest number I have ever heard of. A lot more than twenteen. We steam into Plymouth, the horn of the ship blasting out, the white ensign flying. There are more humans waiting for us here in Plymouth than anywhere else we have docked.[94] Lots of them all lined up, some of them looking very smart, but all of them shouting, calling, waving. Some of them are waving tiny white cloths like small versions of the one my claws got stuck in. It is very, very loud, almost as loud as the Chinese firecrackers.

McCunnell and Gurns, French and Hett, Atkins and Sharpe are standing up on the bow. All the sailors are wearing their blue hats or their white hats. It reminds me of Captain Griffiths's hat. I mewl when I think of Captain Griffiths again, and then yawn when I think of his hat. The sailors are waving, waving down and some humans, who look like old girl-brothers, are shouting and waving right back. George is smiling too.

'So this is home,' he says to me. 'I hope you like it.' He lifts up my front port paw to wave at the humans. I am glad we are getting off,

---

[94] HMS Amethyst docked in Plymouth to a tumultuous welcome on 1st November, 1949, having set sail from Hong Kong in September, after the ship had been repaired.

but I am tired, tired. I don't want any more sunshine, I don't want another human who I don't know to say hello to me. I just want to be with... who I love.

The ship docks with one last blast of the horn and I am deafened by the roar of the crowd. The big tongue is laid down. Not long now until I can get off. I wait for George to pick me up, but it doesn't happen. Instead, two very important looking men come on board and shake hands with Kerans.

'That's Admiral Lord Fraser and Lord Hall,' I hear George say.[95] But only just, because it is still very noisy. Then even more humans come rushing onto the ship. Hang on; this is the opposite of what I want to happen. Girl-brothers looking fresh and clean and some looking not so fresh and clean are hugging all my friends. Everyone has wet eyes. I am surrounded by... humans.

But no one hugs me.

And then... and then... a man walks up to me. He is carrying a huge bag.

'Able Seacat Simon,' and he stands up straight, bangs his feet together and puts his starboard hand to his head. 'For you.' He opens the bag and pulls out lots and lots and lots of... I don't know what they are. Papers with squiggly lines on; tins of I-don't-know-what; small cloth creatures that look a bit like Peggy's smelly old monkey. What am I supposed to do with these?

'The whole world loves you,' he says.

I think I should purr, but I don't. I just think of those who love me, but who aren't here.

Finally, all the girl-brothers and my friends line up to go down the big tongue. Arm in arm, hand in hand. Off they walk. I look round for George, but I cannot see him. More and more sailors are getting off the ship; it is getting emptier and emptier. From nowhere, the man who showed me all of the I-don't-know-whats hands me a saucer of something white to drink. I give it a lick. It is... OK.

---

[95] Admiral of the Fleet, Bruce Austin Fraser, 1st Baron Fraser of North Cape (1888 - 1981). Saw action in the Gallipoli, took part in the internment of the German High Seas Fleet at the end of World War II, served in WWII as Third Sea Lord and Controller of the Navy, Commander of the Home Fleet and assisted in establishing NATO. Viscount Hall - the First Lord of the Admiralty.

And then, I look up… and no one is left on the ship except me. I am happy and I am sad. At least no one is flashing sunshine at me, but there is no one to stroke my head either. What shall I do now? Shall I look for rats? Are there any rats left to catch? I stretch out and lie on the deck. Ouch! My back. I forget it still hurts sometimes. This is the first time I have been on my own. First there was JoJo and then there was Peggy, George and the sailors. I know they will come back though, so I still feel a little bit more good than bad.

From where all the sailors and humans are gathered down below, I hear a huge, booming voice.

'Well done Amethyst. Up to standard.'[96]

I run up to the bow again and look at them all down below. They all look happy, which means that this is happy. So maybe I should just be happy and wait here on this ship. I am looking forward to home.

Wherever that is now.

---

[96] Part of the welcoming speech given to the HMS Amethyst sailors on their return to Plymouth by the First Lord of the Admiralty and the Commander-in-Chief, Plymouth, Admiral Sir Robert Burnett.

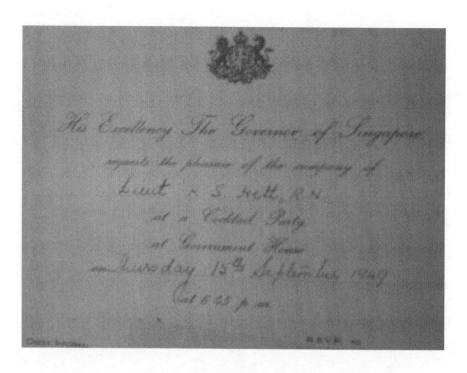

Singapore cocktail party to which the crew were invited – September 1949
Photo courtesy of Lieutenant Commander Stewart Hett

24/ Not flying but moving

After all the sailors had gone I was looking forward to giving myself a nice old lick and clean. I was just about to settle down when the man who gave me the saucer with something white in crept up behind me, scooped me up and put me in a box. It is smaller than Peggy's, seems to be made of the same thing as the deck of the ship that makes my claws go clack, clack, clack and has bars on the front. I can look through the bars and just about put a paw through if I try, but I cannot move around very much. When the man first put me in the box and carried me off the ship he spun me round a bit too fast and it made me feel dizzy. I didn't feel like I was flying; I just felt as if I was caught.

Then he put me and the box in a car. The car coughed and now we are rattling along - bump, bump, bump. I have never been in a car before. I don't like it. Not at all. The car makes this box move around and, every time it bumps, I bump my head on the top of the box. I don't know which I like least - the car or the box. I feel as if my whole world has disappeared. Before, I was on the big, big sea on a huge, huge ship and now I am here in a tiny box in a little car.

I don't know where we are going. I suppose we must be going to George's. I think about where he might live and wonder what it must look like and smell like. Will he have a garden as big as the one Peggy used to run around and play in? I wonder what Peggy is doing now. I suppose she will be eating, wagging her tail and chewing her monkey. Peggy was *my* monkey and I miss her.

What will all the sailors do now? Will they go home with the humans who came to meet us on the ship? Even though a lot of them had wet eyes they all seemed very happy. I wonder if there are any cats who live where George lives. Or dogs. I hope they are as nice and friendly to me as Peggy. I know I can't run very fast now. My back hurts a lot too. Bump! Ouch!

George must live a very long way away from the ship. I cannot see out of the windows of the car, so I don't know what outside is like. I know it felt colder as we docked, but I wonder what sort of creatures they have here. Maybe cats or dogs don't live here. Maybe it is full of the scary monsters that were in Singapore. I feel myself pushed right up against the box as the car turns hard starboard. It can't be very far away now. Not long now before I am back with George.

I feel like I did when I sicked up some pilchard back on the ship. I don't want to be in this box anymore. Where is George? Where does he live? I am not scared because I know it won't be long now, but I feel all trapped and strange. Like a rat in a box. More bumping. I try to close my eyes, but all the movement makes my head spin. Then I try to lie, but I keep sliding around. I try to give myself a lick, but I can't do that either. I mewl, but the man doesn't say anything. Not long now.

Finally, after a long, long time, the car stops. Phew. George really must live very far away from where the ship docked. Why didn't the ship just dock nearer to where he lived? I am hungry. I am not hungry. The car door opens and I am slid along, and then up and out of the car. Don't spin me round too fast! I hear the crunch of the man's footsteps as we walk up to George's big, big house. There are lots of lights on. He must have invited lots of other humans over to see me. So long as they don't make my eyes go blind...

The man opens a door and we walk in. It is very bright. Like sunshine. It hurts my eyes a little. I see some chairs all lined up and pictures of cats on the walls, but no George. Oh well, he is probably making me some lovely food. The man lifts me up and places me on what looks like a counter. It smells all clean in here. I can see a girl and another human. The girl looks at me and smiles. She has black hair and red lips. She puts her fingers through the bars.

'Welcome, Simon. I've heard so much about you. Read about you too.'

George must have told her all about me. I wonder if this is George's girl-brother. I peer out at the pictures of the cats on the walls. Who are they? Why didn't George tell me about them? The clean smell and the bright light and all the cats looking at me make me feel lightheaded. This new place with these new humans is strange. It makes me feel strange. The man behind the counter turns around. It's Pauloni! I'm sure it is. What's he doing here? That must mean everybody is here! I mewl again because I really want to get out of this box now. George! George! Where are you?

'Thanks for bringing him,' Pauloni says. Only his voice is different. He has a different voice to when he normally speaks. Why doesn't he say hello to me? Or give me a titbit?

'We'll just get him checked out now,' and I hear a click and Pauloni's hands reach inside to pull me out. His hands are different to what I remember. I don't like this Pauloni speaking in a different voice. Everything feels strange. I still feel dizzy. I scratch Pauloni's hand. I don't mean to.

Pauloni removes his hand from the box. 'Think we've got a fighter here. Perhaps you can do the honours?'

And then the girl steps forward and reaches inside. I smell her and I feel her hands around me. They are soft and warm. I let her lift me - ow, careful with my back - out of the box and onto the counter. I sit down and look around. Where is he?

The girl smiles at me. 'My name's Molly. We just need to check you over and then you can go and rest. Haven't you had a long journey?'

Yes. Ten thousand miles, George said. And then all the way from the ship to George's home. I'm tired. Yet I cannot sleep because Molly and the Pauloni man prod me and turn me over and pull my ears and lift up my tail. They make lots of squiggly lines on paper and stick something up my bottom and sting me in my side like those yellow and black buzzy things. If this is a hello, I would rather they said goodbye.

Molly takes me into a room. A room that George still isn't in. She places a bowl of the white stuff for me to drink and fetches a tin. I recognise the picture on it straight away. How did she know? Maybe George told her how much I like it, so she got some for me specially. I like Molly.

After I have eaten, Molly takes me outside to a little garden.

'OK, here you can come and play two times a day, but you can't play with any of the other cats yet.'

So there are other cats here? That's nice. I wonder how many there are. So that means I will have lots of new friends as well as George. How strange that I'm not allowed to play with them yet. Maybe they have heard what I did to the rats and they are scared of me. It might not feel so good at the moment, but I know it will soon all be good, good, good. I run around and sniff. Yes, I can smell other cats. I can't smell George though.

Then Molly lifts me up. One of my legs dangles down. She must be taking me to George now. First he picked me up and took me onto the ship and now Molly is taking me to him and doing the same thing. How funny. We go back into George's house from the garden, walk past the counter and go through another door. I close my eyes. I want to hear George say, 'Hello, Simon,' before I open them.

But he doesn't say hello. Nobody says hello. Instead, I hear a clang and feel my paws land on something hard. I open my eyes and turn around quickly. More bars, with Molly's face peering at me from the other side of them.

'There's a good cat.'

The bars clang shut. I am trapped and alone again.

25/ Time to go home

When can I leave here? When will I stop hurting?

'There, there.' Molly is stroking me. 'Can't you have just a little bit more? Just a little bit?'

But I don't want to eat any more Whiskers. This is not home. This is a place called quarantine and I don't want to *be* here.[97] George has seen me a few times. He said he and my other friends went to something called a gala dinner in a place called the Dorchester Hotel. It means that they ate lots of food. I wish I had been there. And all of them marched to somewhere called the Admiralty Church in London where they met the Lord Mayor.[98] I know who the Lord Mayor is. Peggy told me about him. The Lord Mayor is called Dick Whittington and he had a cat who was very good at catching rats. Like me. Like I used to be.

George says I have to stay here for six months and then after that I can go and live with Kerans. Every time he comes he says, 'Not long

---

[97] Simon was taken to quarantine in Surrey. Several of the sailors came to visit him there.

[98] On 16th November, 1949, the Amethyst's crew took part in the Service of the Thanksgiving in St Martin in the Fields, traditionally the 'Admiralty Church', over whose portico flies the Ensign presented by the Lords Commissioners. The service followed the inspection on the Horse Guards Parade. The streets were filled with people paying tribute to the sailors. After singing the hymn 'Now thank we all our God', the vicar, the Reverend L.M. Charles Edwards, read the Naval Prayer, which was followed by a short hymn and the blessing. The crew then marched to a luncheon reception given in their honour by the Lord Mayor of London.

now.' I feel like I have been here a long, long time, but Molly says it hasn't even been four weeks yet. I don't know why I am here. If this is what happens after you have been brave then I wish I hadn't been brave. I was happier when I was scared all the time and I had George to look after me.

I can't wait to go and live with Kerans, although I hope I still get to see George too. Six months is a long time to wait though, I think. I'm not sure how many times I'll see the moon in six months. I don't understand why I can't live with George or Kerans now, just like I used to. I know I am good, I know I have not been bad, so why do I have to be here? Maybe it is just the unlucky part of me after I have been so lucky for such a long time. So if lucky means good and unlucky means bad then maybe there really is some bad in me after all?

Kerans has been to see me. He told me a story about going to a place called the Duke of Cornwall Hotel with Admiral Fraser and some other important people. He said he told them all about me and how they all said how brave and special I was. I don't feel brave or special now. Kerans says that Hett has been appointed Cat Officer as so many people know about me.[99] Whenever he comes to see me he always brings a bag and shows me presents that humans have sent me from around the world. More paper with squiggly lines, red creatures, black creatures, yellow creatures, more food. If I really were magic I would make it so that, when he opens the bag, Peggy would come out. Or JoJo of course. Kerans tells me how the world loves me, but I don't feel loved. I just feel left and alone, so I don't even put my paw through the bars to touch and feel what he has brought me.

But as well as my friends, there've been lots of not friends who have come to see me too. They wanted to give me things and smile and make me blind. Molly said they have come from many different places to see me, but I don't know which ones. When they first started to come I would mewl and it would make me happy, but the more they came the more I just wanted to be with those who I love. Ouch! That was my back again. I do not feel good. Maybe that was the bad? All I can do is wait, but I am tired of waiting. I waited for a long time when we were stranded and now here I am waiting again. To be rescued. To escape.

I do like Molly though. She feeds me and strokes me and she smells of outside. We go out into the garden too. I sniff around, but I have

---

[99] Simon received as many as 200 letters and parcels daily including cards, letters, poems and food.

already explored it lots of times. I know what's over there, so I know there are no holes in the fence for me to squeeze through. There aren't even any rats to catch, so mostly I just sit and look up at the grey sky peeping through the trees above and wish I could fly away. I would fly away from all this grey, all this cold, this horrible quarantine until I found the sea, then I would look for the Amethyst and I would land on it.

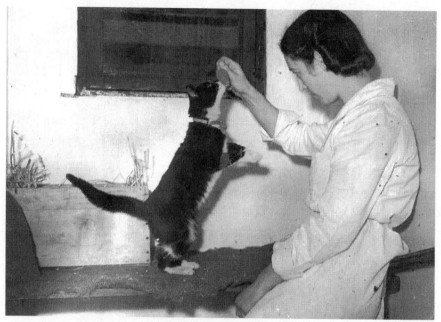

Simon in quarantine with one of the kennel maids
Photo courtesy of the PDSA

I would find Peggy in her box with her monkey and we would both run and hide and play. Maybe I should have stayed with her in the place where I am from? I am not from here and I don't want to be. I am hurting again. I hurt when I close my eyes and I've started to see even more pictures. I hurt when I try to give myself a clean.

I hear the ring of the doorbell. That means someone is here. Molly stands up.

'I'll just go and see who it is,' and she steps out of the little room.

'Simon,' she calls when she steps back in. 'Visitor for you.'

I look up and see George. I want to jump up, but instead all I can do is slowly stand. I am hurting a lot. I give George's fingers a quick sniff. He smells different.

'Hey, Simon.'

I purr at him. Molly is standing next to George.

'How does it feel to be the world's most famous cat?' George smiles at me.

It feels lonely.

'How has he been?' George turns to Molly.

'I think he wonders why he can't leave with you or one of his other friends,' Molly says to him then looks at me. 'Poor little fella.'

'Well. I've got some good news for you,' George smiles at me.

Good news at last! What is it?

'They've arranged a ceremony for you on the 11th of December. That's only two weeks away. You're so famous that Maria Dickin will be there to award you your medal herself. *And* the Lord Mayor.'

The Lord Mayor? How exciting! I hope he brings his cat. I might have someone to talk to, not like these other cats in here with me.

'We'll all be there too of course. Be just like old times.'

I would like to be with everybody again. I would like to see Gurns and all the others. We would not be on the ship of course, but we could just pretend instead, at least for a little bit. Molly walks out of the stuffy room.

'Oh, I've brought you this as well. I found it earlier.' George reaches into his pocket and pulls something out. It is the die. I sniff it. I sniff and sniff. I am sure I can smell Peggy on it.

'You know, Simon,' he says after a while. 'It's the 27th of November today. That means it's been seven whole months since we got into all that bother.'

I try to understand what he is saying. A month is... some moons. Seven is... wait. One, two, three, four, five, six... seven. That means I only have to wait for another few lots of some moons before I can leave here. My heart thuds a little. So, it's been seven whole months since I saw that horrible green glinting eye? I try to think about if that feels like a long time or not. Does that mean it is still a long time for me to stay here until I can leave? I don't know. Thinking about the time George first rescued me seems like moons and moons ago. But as he sits here with me now it does not feel like moons and moons ago at all. My head hurts.

He stands there and looks at me for a while. It hurts to meet his eyes so I have to close mine. I open them a moon or a minute later, but he is gone. My eyes flicker again and George is stroking my head. My back hurts, something hurts, everything hurts. George has been here a long time, for many moons. George has just walked in. His voice snatches me back from there to here.

'I have to go now. But only two weeks. Two weeks, Simon, until your big day. But I'll be back before then.'

And then he is gone. George is here, he is gone.

Later on, after Molly has tried to feed me some more Whiskers, I am out in the garden. It is night time. I look up at the moon. I wonder if it is the same as the one I saw many times on the ship. The same moon that I will see and then not see and then see again until George or Kerans comes and gets me and I can leave here. I am looking forward to that. A lot.

I am just about to go back inside to play with my die and give it another sniff when I suddenly feel all like when I played that nice game with Lilette. No, it is like when I killed all the rats. I want to... I don't know what I want to do. I want to... walk over here. No, I want to go and lie over there. No, I want to... I don't know. I mewl and mewl again. I am burning. The hurt is getting bigger. It is taking over. Taking over me.

'Hey, Simon, what's all the noise about?'

I can feel soft hands pick me up, up.

'Come on fella, let's get you inside.'

Gentle hands which must be Molly's. We must be going back inside because it goes from dark to light. I want to scratch these hands. I want to be comforted by these hands.

'That's it. Let's get you nice and comfortable. My, your nose is hot.'

Where are we now? I can't really see. Things have faded to dark, maybe the lights have broken like they did back on the ship. I am still with Molly. I feel her soft voice. Should I mewl? Would it hurt if I did? Did I mewl just then? I am standing up now, or maybe I am lying on my back. I am standing upside down. Is that Molly?

'OK, OK, Simon. Settle down. Just try and lie still. I think I'd better ask the vet to come and take a look at you, hadn't I?'

No, not Molly, it's George. George is here. I am with George at his house. I have never been here before, but it smells of him. It does have a garden, much bigger than the garden here where I am now. But now Molly is here, not George. Yes, it is Molly. And I'm in the small garden again.

'Right, hang on in there Simon, the vet's on his way. You just hold on, there's a brave chap.'

A vet? A Hett? I roll round and round under and over here. And there. The garden gets bigger as I run and roll and leap and... BANG! I crash into the side of my cage. What's my cage doing out in the garden? Suddenly the garden lights up, bright, bright.

'Now Simon, how's the bravest cat in quarantine doing? Oh dear, you don't look your usual self at all. Let's see what we can do about that, shall we?'

I am back in my box. Peggy had a box. Where is Peggy?

'His temperature has soared and his heart rate is very low.'

My back is... something is on my back. Is it Chairman? I can walk... no, I can't walk... over there... my back... I see monsters... I am scared. I am burning.

'Just stay still for me, Simon. You'll just feel a little scratch.'

I feel a sharp, sharp pain and my insides go all cold. Molly is back. She strokes my ears.

'Shh, shh. Good boy, Simon. Brave boy.'

I am hot and cold. I am happy and sad. I am awake. I am sleeping. I am scared. I am brave. I am alone.

'Right, Simon, I'm going to leave Molly to look after you for a while. You rest well, old chap, and show us all why they're giving you that medal, all right?'

The bright lights suddenly fade, enough for me to open my eyes a little. I take a look around, forgetting where I am or where I want to be. The need to make things go fast, fast has disappeared. I am not hurting anymore. I feel Molly's hands around me.

'Thought we'd lost you there for a moment.'

I am not lost. I know where I am. Somewhere I don't want to be. I can feel water drop onto my back. I didn't know it could rain inside. But I am not inside. I am in the garden. The warm sunlight eases the pain a little, and I find I can slowly stand. Slowly, I pad over to where I want to be. Where I think I want to be. I look up and see Molly's face. Her eyes are all wet like George's.

'Simon? Simon? Where are you going? No, don't do that. Just settle. You'll be OK.'

But I don't feel OK. I feel the... ossopite of OK.

'Please. Stay awake, Simon. Oh, please...'

I am surrounded by shadows, dark faces and fingers that reach out and try to grab me. Fingers that are reaching out through thick, black smoke. Fingers that turn into hands. Hands that belong to Molly. She is holding me, squeezing me tight and I am falling, falling away from her. I hear her crying, more wet dropping onto my head - thud, thud, thud - and on my nose. I taste salt, blink and look around. I am back on the ship. I am on the ship with George and Gurns, Ginger and Atkins. Where is Molly? George's eyes are wet. They are always wet, but he is smiling, smiling down at me.

'You're such a brave cat... '

I cannot lift my head. It is too hard. I see George and the others walking away. Please don't go. Please don't leave me. I'm sorry. I'm sorry for being brave. My paws are too heavy to move them. I try to run after George, but he is getting more small and more small. I am heavy. I am scared. I am alone.

'How about some water, Simon? Come on, just a little, you're dreadfully hot.'

Hot, hot. Bright and hot. The birds are screeching. It must be too hot for them. Everything is hot. Uboat must be hot too because he is standing in a shadow. Uboat!

'Come on,' he is saying. I can hear him.

'Come and play. We can have so many adventures.' Oh, I am so happy to see him. We are running, running away from the hot and towards the big, cool, blue sea.

'So many things, so many things,' he is saying and we are running fast side by side and now we are swimming, swimming. Whales are all around us, the cold water, the hot of Uboat's fur. Where is he? Where's he gone? There he is. I jump onto his back, but he slips through my paws.

'I told you,' he says, 'I told you,' and he runs through the water and runs and runs and goes and goes...

'Come on, Simon. It's OK. Everything will be all right.'

Yes, everything will be all right. I am hurting. I am not hurting. And now Lilette is here. Lilette is here, telling me everything will be all right. In a garden, in a lovely green garden that looks just like the sea. Full of flies dancing around and Lilette is rubbing her head against mine. I can smell her; her smell is all around me, everything will be all right. All I can see is white, the white of Lilette's fur.

'I'm glad you said hello,' she licks me. 'Hello, hello, hello.'

The screaming pain has gone because Lilette is here. I try to run towards her, but my paws won't do what I tell them to, but it doesn't matter because I am here with Lilette.

'Let me brush you,' she says. She is smiling and I am being stroked and brushed. That's nice, I feel safe, my back is being stroked, stroked by Lilette...

'Ssh, ssh, Simon. Everything's OK, don't you fret now. Hang on in there, boy.'

This garden, this lovely peaceful garden, but if I'm in a garden then someone else should be here. I look around and there she is. Oh, why didn't I see her before? Silly me, I should be able to recognise that lovely, wobbly shape anywhere. I'm surprised I didn't smell her. Dear, sweet Peggy stepping out of the shadows. She is not in the shop, she is here with me, where she should be, in the garden.

'Come on now. You can do it, Simon. You keep going, boy.'

Now is all we have, now is all I am. 'Everything is all you are.' Peggy is licking me, we are in her box in the garden.

'No more rats,' she is saying. 'Getting rid of all those rats and now we can have lots of lovely food.'

Yes, lovely food now. Peggy and me can eat and then run and play, running around this garden. I am chasing her.

'You're a dog,' I call after her.

'And you are a wonderfully brave cat.'

Bravely wonderful, full of wonder. I am back, back with Peggy, Pelly, Peggy in a garden on the ship. If she runs, I will follow her. I don't want her to leave me again.

'Let's go to the Raffles Hotel,' she says and we run across the garden, Peggy in front of me, dear old Peggy who I always had to slow down with because she is wobbly and now here she is and I am running, running to catch up with her, across the deck and up to the bow and into her box and she is not there. No! No, come back Peggy. Please.

Where is Peggy? Where is Lilette? Where has Uboat gone? They are not in the box, but they must be. They must be somewhere. They *must* be. I have seen them. I know what is pretend and what is real and this is real. It is.

'Come on, Simon, what'll that crew do without you, eh? Just think of them. Think of that medal. Two weeks, Simon, come on, only two weeks.'

I look around for them all. They must be here somewhere. Where are they hiding? What game are they playing? Are they over here? I walk – I think I walk – over to the corner of the garden. No, not here, but I know they are somewhere. They must be. I have seen Lilette. Seen Uboat and Peggy. The crew must be here. George must be here. Come to take me with him.

'His heart rate's slower still, and the tremors are getting worse. I can't control his temperature anymore. I don't know what else I can do.'

I look in the box. I look all around the box. Where are they? Maybe if I just lie here next to the box then they will appear again. I don't know where else to go. They can come and find me, if I just lie here behind this box and wait. I don't know where else to go or what to do. I am alone.

'Titch?'

No! It can't be, can it? Yes, yes it is. It's JoJo! He is walking towards me. He has not stopped! He is moving, moving right towards me. He is here.

'Oh, JoJo! JoJo! I've missed you so much. I have so many stories... '

'I know you do. You are such a wonderful little brother to have. You've done so many things... '

He looks the same, he smells the same, he *is* the same. Where has he been? It is so lovely to have him back. Now I can show him the ship and he can meet George. We can run around on the ship and slip around in the soap suds and play with the die. I want to show him the things I can touch but cannot see. I want to tell him about that silly man, Henri, with his clicky, clicky thing that kept hitting my nose.

'Oh, JoJo, I was so scared when there were all those bangs on the ship.'

'Yes, but don't be scared now. There's nothing to be scared of. You're so brave.'

JoJo is standing in a shadow. What did Peggy say about shadows? That sometimes they are good and sometimes they are bad. Well this is good, good, good. It is not scary. There are no monsters here. It is just those who I love, here in the place where I am not from and a place I won't *be* in for very long either.

JoJo? JoJo? Where's he gone? I look around, but I cannot see him. No! No! No!

'Keep fighting, Simon. Show us all that brave spirit that everyone's talking about.'

Molly stops speaking. I hear her crying. It makes me sad. Please don't cry, Moggy.

I feel scared again. Scared and alone. Where are they? Where have they gone? I don't want to be alone. Please don't let me be here all alone. I don't even know where here is anymore. I am not on the ship, I am not in the garden, I am not in a box, I am falling, I am here, I am getting more small and more small, I am frightened.

I am on my own.

I feel like it is raining even more hard on my head. I whimper and hear a sob and soft hands slip away from round me.

'I think that's it. He's comfortable now. We've done all we can.'

And then. And then... A shape. Who is it? What is it? I don't want to be here. The shape gets more close and more close. It is black and it is white. Then I see who it is. I know who it is. Yes, I would rather be here. I am not scared. I am not alone. It's mother! My mother.

'All right, brave boy. Rest now.'

My mother gives me a lovely lick and cuddles right, right up to me. She is lovely and warm and soft.

'Come now.' She sounds as if she is very far away. 'I'm here. Nothing can harm you now.'

'Oh mother, mother. I wish you had never left me.'

'I've never left you, you silly boy.'

'You did! You left me. Then JoJo left me. I hid, I was so scared. I was shaking.'

'Not all of you was shaking. Your tail—'

'You mean...?'

'Yes,' she nuzzles me. 'I was always there. Helping you.'

She cuddles me. I am warm. I am safe.

A cold breeze ruffles my fur. The garden is disappearing. I can no longer hear Molly.

'Will it...? Will everything...? Is it all going to be OK, mother?'

'Yes. Yes, you are with me now. Come rest against me, feel my fur against yours.'

I'm purring now. So happy. I feel no pain. Just the gentle rise and fall of my mother beside me, her warm body enveloping mine, her tail wrapped around me. I hear nothing but her soft voice.

'We have to go now.' She cuddles me. I am protected. I know where I am from and where I am not from. I know I have to go away. My mother is comforting me, soothing me. I hear her, far away, yet more close, close, close.

'It's time.'

My eyes are open. The sky is bright. I wish I could fly away. I close my eyes. I can smell her, feel her, hear her. I am not in quarantine anymore. I am here. Where I belong. I am surrounded by my mother, by her warmth, by her breath. I think I really know what love is now.

My mother's face right up, up, close, close to mine. I gaze into her soft, round eyes and her whiskers touch mine.

'Come on now, my beautiful boy,' she smiles at me. For the last time. For the first time.

'Let's go home.'

Epilogue

Simon died on the 28th of November, 1949. George was the last of us to see him. He had visited Simon the night before to tell him the news about the award ceremony. A vet was sent for that night as the poor little thing had acute enteritis and a high temperature. The vet gave him an injection and some tablets but, sadly, he didn't make it through. He was only about three years old too but, if truth be told, I don't think he ever really recovered from when we were attacked.

Simon was such a wonderfully brave cat that he was awarded the Blue Cross Medal and the Amethyst Campaign Ribbon too, not just the Dickin Medal from the PDSA.[100]

I am so glad George found Simon. Sorry - Able Seacat Simon - on Stonecutters Island when he did. I know I didn't much take to him when he first appeared, but he fair old cheered me and the others up, he did, 'specially when we were stranded for all that time. And as for the rats! I really don't know what we would have done without Simon, particularly when he killed that blasted Mao Tse Tung. Huge bugger, it was. We all had a go at catching him, but it was Simon who finally did.

---

[100] The Blue Cross was founded in London in 1897. Medals have been awarded to animals that have demonstrated bravery or heroism.

We were all really upset when George told us the news about Simon's death. He was such a comfort to us men on board. And all the cards, letters and flowers the quarantine shelter received after he'd gone! Even more than when he was still alive. Old Hett ended up being appointed Cat Officer to deal with it all. Simon even had an obituary in Time magazine too; you can't say that about too many cats can you? In fact, I'm not sure you can say it about any others.

Anyway, when the sad day of Simon's funeral service came, his body was wrapped in cotton wool, placed in a specially made casket and draped in a Union Flag. We had a short ceremony held by Father Henry Ross, the rector of St Augustine's church, and he was buried at the PDSA's animal cemetery in Ilford, East London with full Naval Honours. Kerans and his wife accepted Simon's Dickin Medal posthumously - unheard of for a Captain and his wife to be doing that for a cat. Such a shame Simon wasn't able to receive it himself.

There's a monument to him there.[101] The inscription reads:

IN

MEMORY OF

"SIMON"

SERVED IN

H.M.S. AMETHYST

MAY 1948 - NOVEMBER 1949

AWARDED DICKIN MEDAL

AUGUST 1949

DIED 28TH NOVEMBER 1949.

THROUGHOUT THE YANGTSE INCIDENT

HIS BEHAVIOUR WAS OF THE HIGHEST ORDER

We were all there that day of course - Kerans, me, all of us. And we felt that Simon was there too. When he was on board our ship he was a wonderful reminder of our friends and loved ones back home, and at his memorial we remembered just how much strength he gave us. And that has stayed with us all, I think.

---

[101] A memorial plaque, sculpted by Elizabeth Muntz, was also unveiled at the PDSA hospital in Plymouth on 13th April 1950 by Lt. Geoffrey L. Weston.

Amongst all the horror we were surrounded by at times, he was a great reminder of just how much good there can be in the world too, no matter where you find it, or how small and furry it is.

We will never forget Simon and I hope you won't forget his story either.

Lest we forget.

Able Seaman McCunnell

The original wooden headstone
Photo courtesy of the PDSA

Message from Jacky Donovan

If you have enjoyed reading *Simon Ships Out: How one brave, stray cat became a worldwide hero* I would be extremely grateful if you could leave a review on Amazon.

I'd also love to hear your comments and am happy to answer any questions you may have, so do please get in touch with me by:

- emailing me via my website www.SimonShipsOut.com

- following Simon on twitter - @HeroicCats

I look forward to hearing from you.

Jacky Donovan

Acknowledgements from Jacky Donovan

My thanks firstly to Patrick Roberts whose website www.purr-n-fur.org.uk formed the basis of my interest in Simon's unique story. He kindly put me in touch with Lieutenant Commander K. Stewart Hett, M.B.E., R.N., Ret. - one of few HMS Amethyst crew still alive today.

I am indebted to Stewart for his helpfulness in addressing the many and varied queries I launched at him whilst writing the book. It was a pleasure to meet him and have access to his extensive archives and I am grateful to him for many of the photographs that appear in the book. However, on behalf of Able Seacat Simon, whose dialogue occasionally takes on a degree of artistic licence, I apologise unreservedly to Stewart for any inaccuracies which ensue in the narrative.

Thanks to Rebecca Stone, granddaughter of Telegraphist 'Bob' Stone who served on HMS Amethyst during the period in question and who sadly died in March 2014. Her research and design for a Narrative Exhibit and Memorial commemorating HMS Amethyst, as part of her BA(Hons) Interior Architecture and Design course at the Arts University Bournemouth, provided me with further useful material. I hope she one day sees her design become reality. www.rebeccastonedesign.tumblr.com

Thank you to the PDSA for taking a look at relevant sections of my manuscript and allowing me to use their archive photos of Simon's story; to Paul McCunnell whose advice about ships was extremely useful; to Dana Rizki Nur Adnan for the cover design and to Lika Kvirikashvili for the illustrations.

I'm grateful to the wonderful readers and authors on facebook group 'We Love Memoirs' for their feedback and engaging participation when I needed to bounce ideas around or just recharge my batteries. I recommend you join them to engage in regular friendly banter about memoirs and life in general. www.facebook.com/groups/welovememoirs

Last, but by no means least, thanks to everyone who helped me get Simon's story into words, enabling me to give a cat's eye view of life on board HMS Amethyst. Your suggestions were invaluable in shaping the book into its final format, thank you.

Further photos

The new headstone at Ilford Cemetery
Photo courtesy of the PDSA

The new headstone at Ilford Cemetery
Photo courtesy of the PDSA

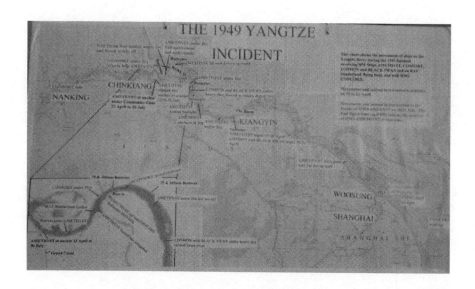

Map depicting the Yangtze Incident
Courtesy of Lieutenant Commander Stewart Hett

Simon Neuter Cat Died before Award
"Served on H.M.S. "Amethyst" during Yangtse incident disposing of many rats though wounded by shell blast. Throughout the incident his behaviour was of the highest order although the blast was capable of making a hole over a foot in diameter in a steel plate."

Simon's PDSA Dickin Medal citation
Photo courtesy of the PDSA

Front of Simon's PDSA Dickin Medal.
Photo courtesy of Eaton Film Company who bought it in 1993.
The medal is loaned out for exhibitions from time to time.

Reverse of Simon's PDSA Dickin Medal.
Photo courtesy of Eaton Film Company who bought it in 1993.
The medal is loaned out for exhibitions from time to time.

HMS Amethyst's company marching through Plymouth – November 1949
Photo courtesy of Lieutenant Commander Stewart Hett

HMS Amethyst's company marching through Plymouth – November 1949
Photo courtesy of Lieutenant Commander Stewart Hett

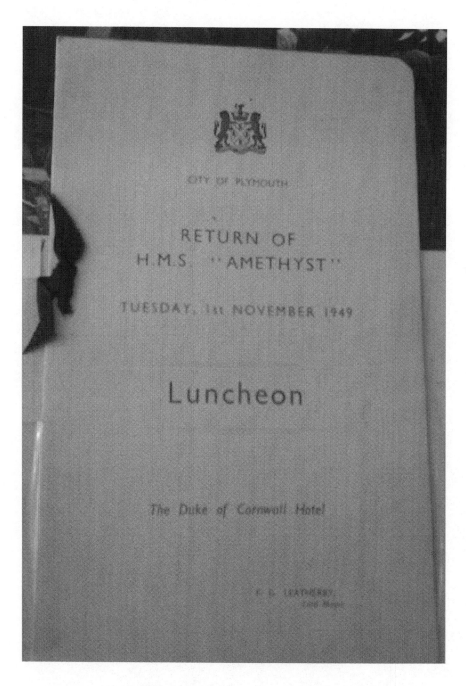

Lunch at the Duke of Cornwall Hotel
Photo courtesy of Lieutenant Commander Stewart Hett

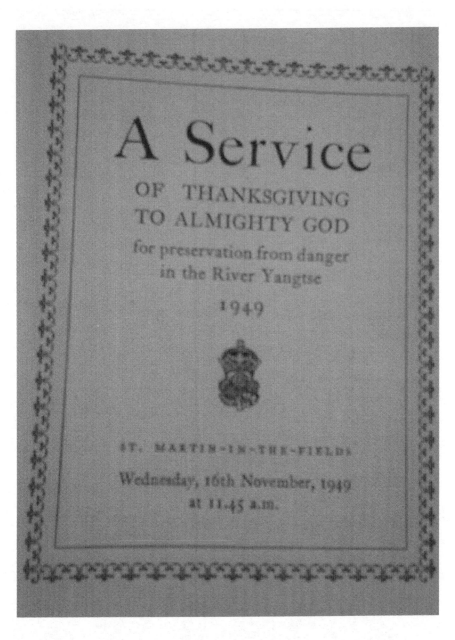

Thanksgiving Service at St. Martin-in-the-Fields – November 1949
Photo courtesy of Lieutenant Commander Stewart Hett

THE CORPORATION OF LONDON

requests the honour of the Company of

Lieutenant K.S. Hett, R.N.

LUNCHEON at GUILDHALL on WEDNESDAY the 16th NOVEMBER, 1949

AT 12.30 P.M. FOR 12.45 P.M.

To welcome the Officers and Men of

H.M.S. AMETHYST

and contingents from H.M. Ships London, Consort and Black Swan,
and the Crew of the Royal Air Force Sunderland Aircraft
engaged in the river Yangtse 1949

The favour of an early answer addressed to " The Town Clerk, 3182, Mansion, E.C2, " is requested

MORNING DRESS OR UNIFORM

Invitation to the Guildhall Luncheon
Photo courtesy of Lieutenant Commander Stewart Hett

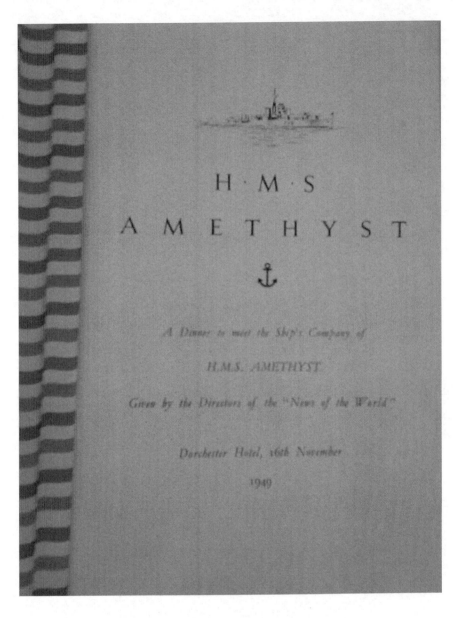

H·M·S

AMETHYST

A Dinner to meet the Ship's Company of

H.M.S. AMETHYST

Given by the Directors of the "News of the World"

Dorchester Hotel, 16th November

1949

Invitation to dinner at the Dorchester Hotel
Photo courtesy of Lieutenant Commander Stewart Hett

Part of Rebecca Stone's exhibition for a Narrative Exhibit and
Memorial commemorating HMS Amethyst
Photo courtesy of Rebecca Stone

'Where's Simon?' is a family friendly and child focused activity embedded within Rebecca Stone's exhibit. Visitors will have to find and follow the cat's silhouette around the exhibit before coming to a designated area that reveals Simon's heroic tale.

Photo courtesy of Rebecca Stone

27th April 2014: Survivors and relatives gather for the 65th Anniversary ceremony in remembrance of the Yangtze Incident at the National Memorial Arboretum, Alrewas, Staffordshire. During the ceremony the names of all those lost were read by Stewart Hett, senior surviving officer of HMS Amethyst. Stewart is seen on the left holding the list.

Photo courtesy of Lieutenant Commander Stewart Hett

27th April 2014: Memorial stone at the National Memorial Arboretum, Alrewas, Staffordshire.

Photo courtesy of Lieutenant Commander Stewart Hett

Ant Press books

If you enjoyed this book, you may also enjoy these titles:

Fat Dogs and French Estates ~ Part I by Beth Haslam

Fat Dogs and French Estates ~ Part II by Beth Haslam

Chickens, Mules and Two Old Fools by Victoria Twead
(Wall Street Journal Top 10 bestseller)

Two Old Fools ~ Olé! by Victoria Twead

Two Old Fools on a Camel by Victoria Twead
(New York Times bestseller x 3)

Two Old Fools in Spain Again by Victoria Twead

One Young Fool in Dorset by Victoria Twead

Instant Whips and Dream Toppings: A true-life dom rom com by Jacky Donovan

Heartprints of Africa: A Family's Story of Faith, Love, Adventure, and Turmoil by Cinda Adams Brooks

How not to be a Soldier: My Antics in the British Army by Lorna McCann

Into Africa with 3 Kids, 13 Crates and a Husband by Ann Patras

Paw Prints in Oman: Dogs, Mogs and Me by Charlotte Smith
(New York Times bestseller)

Joan's Descent into Alzheimer's by Jill Stoking

The Girl Behind the Painted Smile: My battle with the bottle
by Catherine Lockwood

The Coconut Chronicles: Two Guys, One Caribbean Dream House by
Patrick Youngblood

Midwife: A Calling (Memoirs of an Urban Midwife Book I) by Peggy
Vincent

www.SimonShipsOut.com